Gulf Coast

LIGHTHOUSES

FLORIDA KEYS *to the* RIO GRANDE

PHOTOGRAPHS *by* BRUCE ROBERTS
TEXT *by* RAY JONES

The Globe Pequot Press

Old Saybrook, Connecticut

To Edith King
—BRUCE ROBERTS

For Harry Claiborne, Winslow Lewis, George Meade, and Danville Leadbetter
—RAY JONES

Sand Island Lighthouse at sunset

Copyright © 1989, 1995, 1998 by Bruce Roberts and Ray Jones
All rights reserved. No part of this book may be reproduced or transmitted in any form by any means, electronic or mechanical, including photocopying and recording, or by any information storage and retrieval system, except as may be expressly permitted by the 1976 Copyright Act or by the publisher. Requests for permission should be made in writing to The Globe Pequot Press, P.O. Box 833, Old Saybrook, Connecticut 06475.

All photographs, unless otherwise credited, are by Bruce Roberts.
Cover and text design by Nancy Freeborn

Library of Congress Cataloging-in-Publication Data

Roberts, Bruce, 1930–
    Gulf Coast lighthouses : Florida Keys to the Rio Grande /
photographs by Bruce Roberts ; text by Ray Jones. — 1st ed.
        p. cm. — (Lighthouses series)
    Includes bibliographical references and index.
    ISBN 0-7627-0183-8
        1. Lighthouses—Gulf Coast (U.S.)—History. 2. Lighthouses—
Gulf Coast (U.S.)—Pictorial works. I. Jones, Ray, 1948-   . II. Title.
III. Series : Lighthouse series (Old Saybrook, Conn.)
VK1024.G85R63   1998
387.1'55'0976—dc21   98-2845
                                          CIP

Front cover photograph: Sand Key, Florida
Back cover photograph: Mobile Bay, Alabama

Printed in Quebec, Canada
First Edition/First Printing

CONTENTS

The Point Isabel Lighthouse, near Brownsville, formed the last link in a 1,700-mile chain of navigational lights stretching from Key West to the Mexican border.

INTRODUCTION

Probably no mariner has ever been happier to see a shore light than Christopher Columbus. One night more than 500 years ago, the explorer peered into the darkness and caught his first glimpse of the New World—the light of a fire dancing on the western horizon. If there was fire, then there was also land, and he would soon find it.

Perhaps the closest we can come to the Columbus experience nowadays is to drive Florida's aptly named Overseas Highway. Linking the southern tip of the Florida peninsula with Key West, this unique roadway reaches more than 130 miles out into the ocean. For long stretches between the low, sandy keys, it spans the open blue-green water. Dolphins and seabirds play in the waves only a few feet from the concrete. Motorists begin to feel like mariners and at night, especially, may imagine they are about to drop off the edge of the earth. Helping to restore their confidence are the navigational lights at Carysfort Reef, Alligator Reef, Sombrero Key, American Shoal, Sand Key, and elsewhere, winking at them all along the way.

The fabled reef lights of the Florida Keys are the first links in a chain of jewel-like beacons forming a 1,000-mile-wide semicircle from Key West to Corpus Christi, Texas. Both on and just off the shores of the Gulf of Mexico stand many of America's most beautiful, historic, and richly storied lighthouses. Often exposed to powerful gales and hurricanes and undercut by galloping erosion, they are also among our nation's most threatened coastal treasures. This is true, in part, because the Gulf of Mexico is like no other body of water on the planet.

HURRICANE ALLEY

Covering 582,100 square miles in a warm blanket of tropical water averaging a mile in depth, the Gulf is enclosed on three and almost four sides by land. Often, however, the shores of the Gulf are not dry land in the usual sense. The swamps, marshes, and barrier islands that line the coasts of Florida, Alabama, Mississippi, Louisiana, and Texas seem undecided as to whether they belong to the sea or the land. In fact, they may change status each time a major hurricane passes through and exposed sandbars and low islands are converted to shoals lurking just beneath the surface. This never-never quality of its landfalls makes the Gulf extraordinarily dangerous to ships and seamen.

And then, of course, there are the storms. The Gulf is known as "hurricane alley" for good reason. More than half the hurricanes that spin northward out of the Caribbean strike land at some point along the Gulf coast. Major hurricanes may strike with winds up to 200 miles per hour and a force equal to several nuclear blasts.

Given a choice, sailors and their ships will run for open water and ride out the storm at sea—better that than be caught in the shoal-strewn, hull-grinding narrows near the land. On the other hand, people on shore may not be able to get out of the way when a big storm comes. Nowadays, coastal areas are usually evacuated well ahead of time. The hurricane comes and goes, destroying millions of dollars worth of property but taking few if any lives. Not that many years ago, however, the storms struck with little or no warning, and there was no time to evacuate coastal residents. In some such instances lighthouses and their keepers saved the lives of more landlubbers than they did of seamen.

Typically peaceful, the Gulf invites quite strolls along sandy beaches, but its nature is not always so gentle.

TWO DAYS OF DEATH IN GALVESTON

Standing in the gallery of his Bolivar Point Lighthouse on the afternoon of September 7, 1900, keeper Harry Claiborne could see clear signs that trouble was on the way. From his high perch, more than 100 feet above the entrance to Galveston Bay, Claiborne looked down on pristine Texas beaches where, on most days, the blue-green Gulf of Mexico wallowed lazily in the sand. But now the mood of the gulf had changed dramatically. Its waters had turned gray and angry, and it pounded the dunes with enormous waves.

Earlier in the week, when Claiborne had gone into the nearby resort town of Galveston to buy a month's supply of groceries, there was already a hint of uneasiness in people's faces. All summer long the hot, humid air of Galveston Island had buzzed with mosquitoes, but now it vibrated with tension. The weather station on the island had received a distressing cable. Trinidad, on the far side of the Caribbean, had been devastated by a hurricane so powerful that few structures were left standing. It was impossible to say where this deadly storm was now, but sailors arriving at Galveston's bustling wharves brought still more troubling news: They told dock workers, saloon keepers, ladies of the night, and anyone who would listen that they had come through "hell" out in the gulf. Somewhere out there lurked a killer hurricane.

At the turn of the century, meteorologists had no radar or computer-enhanced satellite photos to help them track weather systems; there was no telling where a big storm like this would strike next. It might drift to the east and vent its fury in the empty Atlantic. More likely, however, it would rush northward out of the Caribbean and into the Gulf of Mexico, following a well-traveled path known to sailors as "hurricane alley." In that case, it would threaten all the gulf states from Florida to Texas.

Chances were slim that the storm would hit any one stretch of coastline, so the people of Galveston had no immediate cause for alarm. But then the wind picked up, and high, wispy clouds shaped like fish scales were seen racing westward over the island. The atmospheric pressure started dropping so fast that the barometer at the Galveston Weather Station seemed to have sprung a leak. Seeing these rapid changes, the Weather Bureau put out an emergency forecast—just one word—and editors of the local paper set that word in very large type for their morning editions: HURRICANE.

Strangely, most people ignored the warning. Some even rode out to the island on excursion trains from Houston to witness the natural spectacle firsthand. Throughout the morning of September 8, larger and larger crowds gathered to watch the huge waves slamming into the Galveston beaches. Children squealed with delight and clapped their hands as the big waves crashed down, throwing frothy spray into their faces. It was a tremendous show.

Seeing the big crowd of spectators gathered on the shore, Weather Bureau meteorologist Isaac Cline could not believe his eyes. Was it possible that these fools were ignorant of the imminent danger they faced? Cline knew hurricanes often generated tides of a dozen feet or more; the town was only eight feet above sea level. It required very little mathematical skill to deduce that a really powerful storm could wash right over Galveston Island and drown everyone on it.

Cline drove up and down the beach in a horse-drawn buggy, shouting at people to go home or, if they could, to get to the mainland. Few listened to him. The twentieth century had arrived, bringing with it trains, steamships, electric lights, and bottled soda. Why should anyone fear a summer storm? Des-

The iron-clad tower of the Bolivar Point Lighthouse provided refuge for a few dozen frightened refugees during the 1906 Galveston, Texas, hurricane and flood that killed thousands.

perately, Cline pointed to the hurricane flags cracking like whips in the wind. But few noticed the flags, even when the gale started ripping them to tatters.

The revelers at the beach would not listen to the plea of a weatherman, but the weather itself soon confronted them with a more forceful argument. A wooden pagodalike structure stretched several hundred feet along a two-block stretch of the Galveston beach. It was used on holidays and weekends as a dance floor and as a boardwalk for strolling lovers. But now the surf was using it as a punching bag. The pagoda began to sag, and within minutes, the waves turned it into a surging mass of driftwood. This calamity finally convinced people that the approaching storm meant business. Much to Cline's relief, the crowd of wave-watchers began to disperse. Those who lived nearby hurried home and nailed up their shutters. Others began to look for ways to get off the island. But for many it was already too late.

At Bolivar Point Claiborne made sure his light had plenty of oil. Its beacon would be needed by ships caught in the storm and seeking haven in the calmer waters of Galveston Bay. The keeper did not know it yet, but the lighthouse itself would soon become a haven for scores of terrified people struggling to keep their heads above a boiling flood tide.

A prosperous seaport and resort, turn-of-the-century Galveston had its share of turreted Victorian palaces. Surrounded by tall palms and oleanders, they lined the handsome boulevards that ran down the spine of the island. But only a few of Galveston's 40,000 residents lived in mansions. Most made do in rundown tenements and shacks clustered on the low, marshy ground near the wharves. It was the poor who first felt the murky flood waters swirling around their ankles. Forced to abandon their meager belongings, they fled toward the center of the island, where the homes of the rich stood on slightly higher ground. But the relentless tide followed, and soon, there was no longer any spot on the island that could rightly be described as dry land. Dozens drowned, then hundreds, then thousands.

The high water was not the only danger. The wind hurled boards, beach chairs, and massive tree limbs through the air. It turned pebbles into bullets and shards of broken glass into daggers. It ripped the redbrick tiles from the roofs of public buildings and sent them spinning through the streets to decapitate or crush the skulls of its hapless victims. To be out in the open meant death.

Driven from his house by the rising water, Claiborne sought safety within the strong brick walls of his lighthouse. But he had barely closed the heavy metal door behind him when people started pounding on it, begging him to let them in. Despite the gale and the fast-rising water now covering the floor of the lighthouse, Claiborne shoved open the door; after all, he was in the business of saving lives.

Before long the tower was crammed all the way to the top with frightened men, women, and children, who clung desperately to the steps and rails of its spiral staircase. More than one hundred people, many of them from a train that had been stranded by the flood, found sanctuary in the lighthouse; Claiborne must have wondered how he could fit in any more refugees. After a while, though, no one else came. In fact, the big door was soon hidden under as much as thirty feet of water.

To save themselves from drowning, people on the lower steps had to clamber over the heads and shoulders of those above. Terror-filled voices cried out in the near-total darkness; some called the names of loved ones, hoping that they, too, were safe somewhere above or below on the steps of the tower.

As the hours passed and the storm continued to rage, the air inside the lighthouse grew stifling and fetid. Muscles and limbs became so cramped that people screamed with pain. Some grew ill and threw up on the heads of those below. But no matter how miserable they were, no matter how awful conditions inside became, no one doubted that things were much worse outside. The wind howled and whistled,

Galveston children wander amongst heaps of wreckage, all that remained of their once-splendid city after the killer 1906 hurricane. (Galveston Texas Flood Stereograph, from Center for American History, University of Texas at Austin)

blasting the tower at speeds of up to 150 miles per hour. Swept along by the flood, the trunks of fallen trees slammed like battering rams into the walls. The tower shook and the staircase quivered, but the old walls, built in 1871, held fast.

People outside the tower snatched safety wherever they could find it, often in the unlikeliest of places. Some climbed palms and clung to the fronds while the wind clawed at them hour after hour. Others grasped the girders of bridges that had been only partially demolished and pulled themselves up out of the flood. Still others hung onto floating boxes and timbers.

Some of the city's solidly built stone mansions stood up to the storm. Pressed together in the upper rooms of these fine old homes were bank presidents and black gardeners, wealthy matrons and Chinese sailors, debutantes and muscular Latin stevedores. The hurricane had blown away all traces of social distinction.

In the heart of the city, a "lighthouse" very different from the one at Bolivar Point also became a refuge from the storm. A high brick wall surrounding Galveston's Ursuline Convent served as a kind of dike to hold back the flood. Nuns pulled scores of helpless storm victims out of the torrent and over the wall to safety. Among those rescued by the nuns was a pregnant woman who had survived by using an empty steamer trunk as a boat. That night in the convent, the woman gave birth to a baby boy who, though he saw nothing of it, had just lived through the greatest adventure of his life.

Sometime during the early morning hours of September 9, the hurricane passed inland toward the dry plains of west Texas, where it dumped the last of its prodigious rains. Having dwindled down to little more than an ordinary thunderstorm, it wreaked no further havoc other than to flood a few gullies and teach a number of lizards and horned toads to swim. But the storm had already done far more than its quota of damage at Galveston.

When the waters had receded sufficiently that the refugees at Bolivar Point could escape their lighthouse prison, they pushed through the tower door into the sunlight. At last they could breathe and stretch their tortured limbs. But they took no joy in their freedom. Confronted by a scene of utter desolation, they huddled together in horrified silence. Buildings had been knocked down, homes flattened, bridges smashed, ships capsized, trains swept off their tracks, entire communities obliterated. But the most shocking sight of all was right there beside them, just outside the door. Piled up around the base of the lighthouse lay dozens of bodies, many of them stripped naked by the flood. It was as if the tower had been a huge tree, and all these unfortunate people had tried desperately to climb it and keep their heads above the flood. They had failed.

Similar piles of bodies could be seen everywhere throughout the ruins of what once had been the bustling city of Galveston. At least 8,000 people were killed by the storm and the flood tide that accompanied it, but many more may have died. The exact number of dead will never be known.

Even after the storm had passed, the survivors still faced much suffering and hardship. The hurricane had knocked down the bridges and washed away the causeways linking Galveston to the mainland. There were no boats; every vessel in the harbor from the largest freighter to the smallest dinghy had been wrecked or sunk. Cut off from the outside world, the city was without fuel, without sanitation, and without medical facilities of any sort. People could find no food, no shelter, and no unpolluted water to drink. And worst of all, something had to be done with all those bodies.

At Bolivar Point Claiborne fed and sheltered as best he could the people who had weathered the storm with him in the lighthouse. He quickly exhausted the month's allotment of groceries he had purchased only a few days earlier. He figured he'd get by somehow.

On the evening after the hurricane, Claiborne trudged up the steps of the tower. By this time he was no doubt approaching total exhaustion, but duty required that he start up his

Lighthouse lenses such as this giant first-order Fresnel still flash warnings to mariners.

NOTICE TO MARINERS.

(No. 9.)

CORPUS CHRISTI LIGHT-HOUSE,

TEXAS.

FIXED LIGHT.

Notice is hereby given that a *fixed light of the natural color* will be exhibited from the beacon at Corpus Christi, at sunset on Thursday, the 10th of February next, and will be kept burning during that night and every night thereafter from sunset to sunrise.

The lantern is on the keeper's dwelling, and the illuminating apparatus is a Fresnel lens of the 5th order, showing a *fixed light*, and illuminating 350° of the horizon.

The keeper's dwelling is built of brick, and is colored white. The focal plane of the light is 38 feet above the ground, and 77 feet above the level of the sea, and the light should be visible in good weather a distance of 14 nautical miles.

The building is at the north end of the Corpus Christi bluff, and the light is intended for local purposes.

By order:

W. H. STEVENS,
Light-house Inspector Ninth District.

GALVESTON, TEXAS,
January 26, 1859.

In order to avoid possibly disastrous confusion, lighthouse officials tried to give mariners plenty of advanced warning of changes in existing lights or the placement of new ones. The lighthouse described in this pre-Civil War notice no longer exists.

light and make sure it had plenty of oil. For crews on the battered ships that had ridden out the storm in the Gulf, the Bolivar Point Light was a welcome sight. It was also a comfort to the citizens of Galveston, who had endured so much during the previous forty-eight hours. Each time the beacon flashed, they were reminded that some things, at least, still worked and that even in the darkest hours, a few safe havens remained.

STORM-DASHED SENTINELS GUARD THE GULF

Stories about the Gulf Coast lighthouses and the storms that have swept over them go back hundreds of years. In 1699 the French established a settlement at the mouth of the Mississippi River, naming it "The Balize," after a French word that means *beacon* or *seamark*. If the French already had a light shining from The Balize at that time, then it predated by more than a dozen years the 1716 Boston Lighthouse thought by most historians to have been the first such structure in North America. In any case, records confirm that a tower was built at The Balize as early as 1721 by the architect Adrien de Pauger, the same man who designed the city plan for New Orleans. When the Spanish took control of Louisiana in 1762, they began construction of a 120-foot pyramid at The Balize, completing it five years later. Gulf storms no doubt extinguished the beacons atop both the French and Spanish structures on many occasions, but they were always relighted.

During the first half of the nineteenth century, the U.S. government embarked on an extensive program of lighthouse construction along the northern and western Gulf Coast. The Coast Guard built five lighthouses in 1831 alone and eight more during the years 1837–39. By the outbreak of the Civil War, at least fifty-nine towers had been erected, but they were never all in use at the same time. Over the years each of them was repeatedly blasted by hurricanes and other tropical storms only slightly less destructive. Many of the lighthouses, their foundations undermined by flood tides or their towers knocked down by the wind, had to be rebuilt or replaced several times.

Yet the Civil War, a storm of human making, took a higher toll of lighthouses than any hurricane in history. Union ships fired cannonballs into them, while Confederate artillery pounded them to keep the Northerners from using them as observation posts. Since the Southern Navy was very small, safe navigation mostly benefited the North. So the Confederates removed lighthouse lenses and other equipment and hid them away, plunging most of the Southern coast into darkness. Cast-iron towers were often melted down by the metal-hungry Southerners and reforged to make rifle barrels and cannon shot. But like a natural storm, the war eventually passed, and within a few years most of the Gulf Coast lighthouses were back in business, warning sailors of danger or guiding them to safe harbor.

Of the more than sixty major lighthouses that once stood on the flat, sandy headlands along the

Sea oats can bend and dance with the wind, but Florida's Cape St. George tower and others like it all along the Gulf Coast must stand and take whatever the sea throws at them.

thousand miles of coastline from the Florida panhandle to the Mexican border, only a few still function. Many are "darkhouses" now, their lights extinguished and replaced by less costly navigational markers. Some are in ruins, and others have disappeared completely, all traces of them having been erased by the wind and sea. Still, dozens of the old towers remain, much to the delight of architects, historians, and the droves of more casual visitors like ourselves for whom a stretch of shore without a lighthouse is like a beach without the sun.

The New Canal Lighthouse once marked an important harbor on Lake Pontchartrain just north of New Orleans. Although the light remains active, the building now serves as a Coast Guard headquarters.

The Key West Lighthouse remains beautiful, even after 150 years of battering by tropical storms.

CHAPTER ONE

Lights of
THE KILLER REEFS
FLORIDA KEYS

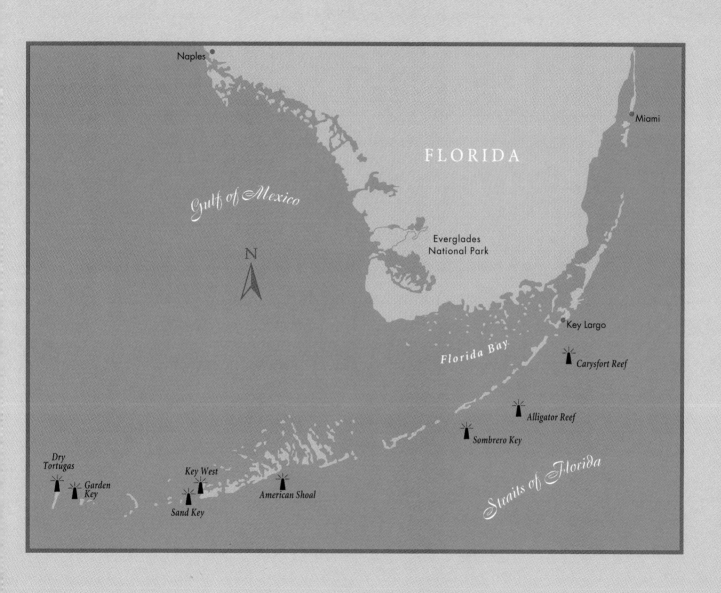

Towering over palms, the Dry Tortugas lighthouse marks the western end of the Florida Keys. (Photo by Bob and Sandra Shanklin)

HAVANA HARBOR, SEPTEMBER 4, 1622

The Armada de Tierra Firme, a large treasure fleet laden with gold and silver from mines in the Andes, is due to sail for Spain. But the senior pilots of the armada are reluctant to take their ships beyond the shelter of the harbor. They know from firsthand experience the perils waiting for them in the Florida Straits: reefs, shoals, shifting sand banks, uncharted islands, and low, barely visible headlands. These are dangerous waters even in the best of weather. And this is hurricane season. What is worse, the signs are ominous: Overhead, clouds race westward, and the wind whistles through rigging as sailors ready the armada for the sea. The waves crashing over the harbor breakwaters grow larger by the hour. The pilots meet with their commander, the Marqués de Caderieta, and beg him not to sail.

But, unlike his pilots, the marqués is not a man of the sea. A nobleman of high rank and reputation, he is proud and fiercely loyal to the king of Spain. The marqués knows the king is anxious to receive this shipment of riches from his possessions in the New World. It must not be delayed by a little wind and rough water. Ignoring the pleas of his pilots, he gives the order to raise anchors.

Despite the choppy seas, the armada makes good progress at first. For two days its big treasure galleons plow eastward through the straits. Meanwhile, the marqués grows increasingly smug and confident that he had made a wise decision in giving the order to sail. Then, on the third day out, the hurricane strikes.

Helmsmen struggle valiantly to keep their vessels on course, but it is hopeless. Raging winds scatter the ships of the armada over a wide area, driving them into the Florida Keys, where reefs and shoals rip open their hulls. Off Matecumbe Key, the 600-ton galleon *Nuestra Señora de Atocha* goes down with most of its crew and more than a million pesos worth of the king's silver bullion. Nearby, the *La Margarita* sinks with almost half a million pesos in silver. In the Dry Tortugas the 600-ton galleon *Nuestra Señora del Rosario* is lost, along with its cargo of precious metals and tobacco. In all, nine ships are wrecked in the Keys. Others are lost, with all hands, on the open sea. A few ships of the armada manage to make it back to Havana. In every case their masts have been snapped off like twigs.

HAVANA HARBOR, JULY 24, 1715

At sunrise a convoy of twelve ships sets sail for Europe. Eleven of the vessels are Spanish treasure ships; one is a French merchant freighter, the *Grifon,* which has received permission to sail with the convoy. Together, the twelve ships carry more than six million pesos in gold and silver, but their cargoes also include South Sea pearls, Chinese porcelain, indigo, cochineal, hides, tobacco, and brazilwood. The Spanish flagship *Capitana* alone carries 1,300 chests brimming with treasure. Also on board the *Capitana* is a small chest filled with jewelry intended to adorn the queen of Spain.

For six days the convoy picks its way slowly up the channel separating the Bahamas from Florida. Then, on the night of July 30, the convoy is hit without warning by a hurricane. Howling out of the east, its irresistible winds drive the ships into the sandy shallows off the Florida coast. Miraculously, the French merchantman, the *Grifon,* outruns the storm and safely reaches the open sea. All the Spanish ships are wrecked, with more than 1,000 crewmen and passengers drowned. Perhaps another 1,500 people survive the disaster by swimming ashore or by hanging onto floating pieces of debris and planking torn off their ships by the storm.

HAVANA HARBOR, JULY 13, 1733

At daybreak a convoy of twenty-two treasure ships called the Nueva España Flota sets sail for Spain. Two days later the convoy runs head-on into hurricane-force winds blowing out of the north. The Flota commander, Don Rodrigo de Torres, orders his captains to hurry back to Cuba. But soon the winds swing around to the south, cutting the ships off from the safety of Havana Harbor and driving them into the Florida Keys. By nightfall all twenty-two ships are wrecked. The total number of lives lost is not known. The total value of the treasure lost is also not known, but one of the wrecked ships, the *Capitana El Rubi,* sunk off Key Largo, carried more than five million pesos in silver and gold. Another, the *Almarita El Gallo,* carried precious metals valued at more than four million pesos.

GULF OF FLORIDA, OCTOBER 22, 1752

A hurricane wrecks more than a dozen merchant ships. Lost are the British merchantmen *Alexander, Lancaster, Dolphin, Queen Anne,* and *May,* the colonial merchantmen *Rhode Island* and *Statea,* an unidentified Spanish man-of-war, and several other unidentified Spanish sailing ships.

GULF OF FLORIDA, JUNE 5, 1816

A series of powerful gales wrecks several U.S. merchant vessels off Cape Florida and in the Florida Keys. Lost are the *Atlas,* the *Martha Brae,* the *Cossack,* the *General Pike,* and the *Zanga.*

SANDY KNIFE IN THE SEA

By the nineteenth century the Florida peninsula, together with the chain of low, sandy islands (known as keys) extending westward from its southern tip, was well established as the world's most formidable navigational obstacle. Countless ships and untold thousands of lives had been lost to its shoals and unmarked headlands. Although entire Spanish fleets were wiped out in storm-driven collisions with the Florida coast, there is no clear evidence that the Spanish ever erected any lighthouses there.

But the United States, which took possession of Florida in 1821, could not afford to be as lax as the Spanish had been in the matter of lighthouse construction. Following the Louisiana Purchase in 1803, the seas around Florida had become the young nation's busiest highway for commerce. Since the great wall of the Appalachian Mountains divided the rich farm and cattle lands of the Mississippi Basin from the populous cities of the East Coast, western produce had to be shipped to market by sea. Timber, grain, and livestock were floated down the big muddy western rivers in flatboats to New Orleans and other ports and then loaded onto sailing vessels for the journey eastward to the U.S. Atlantic coast or to Europe.

The voyage invariably took merchant ships around the southern tip of Florida, and every year the treacherous Florida coasts exacted a heavy toll of ships, crews, and cargoes. Wrecks occurred with such regularity that salvaging lost cargo grew into a major industry. A thriving town, almost entirely supported by the salvaging business, took root on Key West. There, dozens of salvaging crews, called "wreckers," worked year-round pulling bales of cotton, loads of lumber, and other valuable goods from the smashed hulls of ships that had run aground off Florida.

Clearly, something had to be done to warn ships away from Florida's threatening shoals and headlands. Most dangerous were the low, sandy keys stretching more than 200 miles southwestward from Cape Florida. Tall brick lighthouses were built on several of the Florida Keys during the 1820s, but these could be placed only on stable islands such as Key West. Vast stretches of waveswept reef and shoal remained unmarked and as dangerous to shipping as they had been during the days of the Spanish treasure fleets. Vessels continued to run aground on the unseen reefs with a tragic monotony, spilling their passengers, crews, and goods into the sea. The problem was not one of negligence. The still young U.S. government had done all it could to warn ships of the Keys' worst dangers. But the technology necessary for building lighthouses on or near the Keys' most dangerous navigational obstacles simply did not exist.

In 1825 one of the nation's first lightships was placed on station at Carysfort Reef, a few miles off Key Largo. This notorious obstacle was named for a shipwreck, that of the British frigate *Carysford*, lost on the reef along with most of her crew in 1770. The reef had destroyed many earlier vessels and, after the *Carysford* disaster, continued to ruin ships at such a rate that several crews of wreckers earned a good living by salvaging their broken remains.

Built in New York the previous year, the Carysfort Lightship sailed southward toward the Keys, but short of its destination took an ignominious detour. The lightship slammed into a reef itself before reaching the one it was supposed to mark. When the crew abandoned ship, a party of unscrupulous salvagers took possession of the vessel and sailed it to Key West, where they put it up for sale. The U.S. government was then forced to buy back its own ship for $10,000.

After finally reaching Carysfort Reef, the lightship's service record continued to be spotty. Its time on station was constantly interrupted: by storms that tore it from its anchors, sometimes driving it aground on the very reef it was intended to guard; by Indians, who attacked crewmen when they went ashore for supplies; and by its own rotten timbers, which put it out of service for good only five years after it was launched. A second ship replaced the original Carysfort Reef Lightship in 1830, and this one served until 1852, when an entirely new concept for marking the Florida Keys came into being.

Many of the lighthouses built early in the nineteenth century were the work of Winslow Lewis, designer of a well-known lamp-and-reflector system for navigational lights. Ironically, Lewis's own nephew was destined to become his chief critic. A government contractor himself, I.W.P. Lewis found fault in his uncle's brick-and-mortar designs for light towers as well as his vaunted optic system, described by some disgruntled mariners as "little more than an ordinary barnyard lantern held in front of a mirror."

Unlike his uncle the younger Lewis saw merit in the sophisticated, though expensive, Fresnel lenses manufactured and sold by the French. Likewise he was fascinated by pile construction techniques and by the possibility of substituting a skeleton of steel supports held rigid by stout cross bracing for the traditional, solid masonry walls of a lighthouse. Young Lewis thought these ideas might make it possible to build lighthouses directly over the most dangerous reefs and shoals in the Florida Keys. At Carysfort Reef Lewis would finally get a chance to put his revolutionary concepts to a rigorous test.

The cast-iron lighthouse at Fort Jefferson was placed in service in 1876, replacing its storm-damaged predecesssor. (Photo by Bob and Sandra Shanklin)

CARYSFORT REEF LIGHT

Key Largo, Florida – 1852

uilt less than a decade before the outbreak of the American Civil War, the Carysfort Reef Lighthouse was the product of a nation caught in a tide of revolutionary change. A 110-foot skeleton of braced steel supports firmly anchored to massive iron pilings, it was a radical departure from traditional masonry light towers. More than a few of the early light towers were built by leg-endary contractor Winslow Lewis, whose patented lamps had burned for decades in lighthouses throughout the United States.

Indeed, Lewis submitted a bid to build the open-water tower at Carysfort Reef. His design called for a conical tower with solid walls of blocked stone resting on a massive caisson. A special government panel rejected the

(Courtesy U.S. Coast Guard)

Winslow Lewis bid, however, opting instead for a plan put forward by the contractor's nephew, I.W.P. Lewis.

As mentioned above, young Lewis was his uncle's harshest critic and archrival. In fact, the two men could not bear to speak to each other and could hardly have been more different. Winslow Lewis had started out as a seaman. His nephew was a trained engineer. The older Lewis represented the era of wooden sailing ships, stone forts, and brick lighthouses, while the younger embraced iron, steam, and mechanization. In 1848 I.W.P. Lewis had compiled a report lambasting the workmanship and maintenance of America's lighthouses. He found both the structures and their lighting systems vastly inferior to their European counterparts. Wasting little avuncular warmth on his nephew, Winslow Lewis furiously defended himself, but to no avail. It was I.W.P. Lewis who now had the ear of Congress and who got the Carysfort Reef Lighthouse contract.

One of the first of its kind, the lighthouse stood—and still stands, almost a century and a half after it was built—on eight cast-iron legs arranged in an octagon some fifty feet wide. Each leg was anchored to the sea bottom by means of a screw pile, a hollow iron shaft with an auger-like bit that was twisted at least ten feet down through the coral and underlying sand. To stabilize the piles they were capped with massive iron discs four feet in diameter.

Braced by iron girds and tie bars, the legs held aloft a twenty-four-foot-wide platform on which a two-story keeper's dwelling was built. A second platform about one hundred feet above the water held the lantern room. Keepers reached the lantern room by way of a staircase rising through a cylinder centered between the outer piles.

I.W.P. Lewis saw to it that the lantern was fitted with a high-quality, first-order Fresnel lens—and definitely not a reflector-style lighting system similar to the one his uncle had invented. Lighted by a whale-oil lamp, the lens emitted flashes seen from up to eighteen miles away.

Begun in 1848, construction of the lighthouse was delayed by funding shortages and foul weather for almost four years. It was finally completed in 1852 by a crew working under the direction of a U.S. Army officer, Lieutenant George Meade. Like I.W.P. Lewis, Meade was an engineer and a child of the new, iron-willed machine age. Meade would later oversee construction of numerous other lighthouses, including those at Sand Key, completed in 1853, and Sombrero Key, completed in 1856. As General Meade, some years later he would find a ray of light in a moment of darkness for his nation by leading the Union forces to victory at Gettysburg.

The Carysfort Reef Light was automated in 1960, but for more than a century a keeper and several assistants were on duty there at all times. Periodically, a tender brought supplies from Key West, and fresh water was kept in a 3,500-gallon tank and several 600-gallon auxiliary tanks. Keepers and assistants remained at the station for months at a stretch. A small library and a checkerboard helped them pass their off-duty hours. During hurricane season there was often more excitement than any of the crew wanted. Since the big storms gave scant warning, crew members could only batten down and hope for the best.

Today the old lighthouse stands guard over the reef alone. Batteries for its electric light are charged by solar panels.

HOW TO GET THERE:

The lighthouse can be seen from CR-905 on Key Largo. To see it up close, however, you must charter a boat in Key Largo and make the several-mile run out to the lighthouse. Visitors are not allowed on the structure itself.

For those seeking the scenic thrill of a lifetime, scheduled air service is available from Fort Lauderdale to Key West, featuring a low-level overflight of the Florida Keys and most of the major reef towers, including the Carysfort Reef lighthouse. For information contact Sky America Airlines at 4707 140th Avenue North, FL 34622; (800) 742-6278.

ALLIGATOR REEF LIGHT

Matecumbe Key, Florida – 1873

ffectionately know as "Old Gator," the Alligator Reef Lighthouse is even tougher than the leather hides of the toothy swamp reptiles that haunt the banks of bayous along the Gulf Coast. Built in 1873 on a waveswept reef off Matecumbe Key, the station has stood up to dozens of major hurricanes and countless gales. Even the 1935 Labor Day superstorm that slammed the iron-skeleton tower with a twenty-foot wall of water could not topple it.

The station has survived a tidal wave of progress as well. The last full-time keepers locked the doors of the elevated dwelling and climbed aboard a Coast Guard relief vessel in 1963. Afterwards the tower was left to stand its nightly vigil alone, but its automated light has remained fully operational. Lamps once fueled by oil or kerosene are now powered by batteries recharged by solar panels, and the light continues to shine each night, flashing white and red at sixty-second intervals. Sailors on ships passing

The watery world of this old skeleton tower features plenty of sharks but no alligators.

through the Florida Keys are always glad to see the beacon. Although they now have radar and satellite-assisted electronics to help them find their way, the light is still needed to guide them safely past one of the world's deadliest reefs.

Despite its playful moniker, neither Old Gator nor the ship-killing reef on which it stands are named for the American alligator. Instead, the names honor the U.S. Navy schooner *Alligator,* sunk here in 1822. The *Alligator* had won a notable victory over a small fleet of pirate ships only two weeks before she went down on the reef in mysterious circumstances. Her own crew scuttled her for reasons that have never been made entirely clear.

Unlike the *U.S.S. Alligator,* most of the vessels that have foundered here—and they may be too numerous to count—have fallen victim to storms or to navigational error. The reef's jagged coral has been tearing open the hulls of ships for hundreds of years. In 1622, exactly two centuries before the sinking of the *Alligator,* the reef chewed up the 600-ton Spanish galleon *Nuestra Señora del Rosario,* spilling a treasury of gold and silver into the sea. In time the Spanish lost so many vessels and crews in this area that they gave the forbidding name *matanza,* or "slaughter," to a small island about four miles from Alligator Reef. To American sailors this island was known as Indian Key, but they held it in no higher regard than did the Spanish. For many years Indian Key was a favorite hideout of the pirates who preyed on the hapless vessels that regularly ran aground on nearby reefs and shoals.

Having taken control of the Keys along with the rest of Florida in 1821, the U.S. government was determined to make them safer for shipping. Military vessels such as the *Alligator* were sent to rout the pirates and surveyors dispatched to locate key obstacles requiring warning beacons. But marking the Keys with navigational lights would be an expensive and time-consuming process. The Keys had been clear of pirates for decades before an adequate system of lights was in place. For many years it was believed impossible to build a lighthouse tower on an open-water reef. The successful completion of the Carysfort Reef Lighthouse in 1852 proved that it could be done by using the new screw-pile construction technique. This feat was not attempted at Alligator Reef, however, until well after the Civil War.

Construction of the Alligator Reef tower finally got underway during the summer of 1870. Ironically, the project headquarters and barracks for the workers was located on nearby Indian Key, then inhabited by wreckers who made their living salvaging vessels that had run onto the reef.

As with the nearby Carysfort Reef Lighthouse, the skeleton tower erected on Alligator Reef stood on iron pilings. These were driven at least ten-feet deep into the coral with blows from a 2,000-pound hammer. Iron discs help anchor the twelve-inch pilings to the coral.

Held back by repeated storms and funding shortages, the work was not completed until November 1873. In all, the project had cost the U.S. government $185,000—not an inconsiderable sum during the nineteenth century. Old Gator has proven well worth its hefty price, however. The 136-foot tower still stands today, as solid as ever.

HOW TO GET THERE:

Those familiar with the Overseas Highway, a unique, 126-mile paved road following the bed of a historic railway that once linked Key West to the mainland, know that it seems to skim just above the ocean's surface. There are more than forty bridges, and too many flat, sandy islands to count. Motorists here may feel they are driving across the open ocean, and that is more or less what they are doing. It is impossible to get lost since there is really only one road, but because of the almost total lack of landmarks, it is also very difficult to determine your location. The best way to do it is to follow the white and green mile markers beside the road.

The Alligator Reef Lighthouse can be viewed from several points along this beautiful roadway. From Mile Marker 80, near the north end of Lower Matecumbe Key, to about Mile Marker 77, motorists may look to the southeast and see the fine old skeleton tower, or at night its bold flashes. To view or photograph the lighthouse at leisure, turn off the road at Mile Marker 79. For information on seeing the light from the air, see the directions for Carysfort Reef Lighthouse on page 17.

SOMBRERO KEY LIGHT

Marathon, Florida – 1858

At Gettysburg in 1863 General George Meade engineered a famous battlefield victory that cost thousands of lives but likely saved the Union. Only a few years earlier, engineer George Meade had supervised construction of several lifesaving lighthouses in the Florida Keys, including the one at Sombrero Key. At the time Meade tackled the daunting task of establishing a permanent navigational light on this remote Florida reef, he was a U.S. Army captain assigned to the Corps of Topographical Engineers.

The tower at Sombrero Key had been scheduled for construction in 1854, but the task confronted Meade with

even greater difficulties than he had faced at earlier open-water sites. Storms repeatedly lashed the key, destroying equipment and driving away construction crews for weeks at a time. Funding shortages brought further delays. The lighthouse was not completed until 1858, but the structure has proven well worth the four years and more than $150,000 it took to build it. Despite continuous pounding by gales and hurricanes, the tower still stands today, more than 140 years after the station entered service.

One reason for the remarkable longevity of the 142-foot tower may be a technical innovation Captain Meade made in its design. Meade knew the reef rose out of the sea at low tide and that this would alternately bathe the foundation in saltwater and expose it to air. It was believed this would cause rapid deterioration of iron pilings and that, eventually, they would fail, causing the tower to collapse under its own weight. To solve this problem, Meade used pilings made of hardened, galvanized steel. As with the other reef lighthouses he built, the pilings were hammered through metal discs and deep into the underlying coral.

The station's original first-order Fresnel lenses cost $20,000 and produced a fixed white light visible from up to fifteen miles away. In 1931 the light was changed from fixed to flashing by fitting the lens with revolving opaque screens. In 1984 the huge Fresnel was removed and placed on display in the Key West Lighthouse Museum. The modern optic that replaced it is powered by batteries recharged by solar cells.

HOW TO GET THERE:

The lighthouse can best be viewed from Sombrero Beach State Park near the town of Marathon on Vaca Key. At Mile Marker 50 turn left onto State 931, also known as Sombrero Road, and follow it approximately 2 miles to the park. Admission is free, but the view, like so many in the Florida Keys, is worth millions. The station's old first-order Fresnel is on display at the Key West Lighthouse Museum. Anyone fascinated by the Florida reef lights or lighthouses in general should visit this excellent museum. For information contact the Key West Lighthouse Museum, 938 Whitehead Street, Key West, FL 33040; (305) 294–0012.

(Photo by Bob and Sandra Shanklin)

AMERICAN SHOAL LIGHT

Sugarloaf Key, Florida – 1880

In February 1744 Captain Ashby Utting ordered his warship, the forty-four-gun British Frigate *Loo,* into the perilous Florida Straits to search for Spanish pirates. Not far from Havana Ashby's lookouts sighted the *Billander Betty,* a British ship that had been taken captive by the Spanish some weeks earlier. The *Loo* pounded away at the enemy with her heavy guns and before long had recaptured the *Betty.* Then, to avoid marauding Spanish fleets that might easily overpower them, the two ships—the *Loo* and the repatriated *Betty*—hurried northward toward safety in the Carolinas. They would never make it.

Although Captain Utting set a course that should have taken the two ships directly up the east coast of Florida, the unpredictable currents drove them northwestward instead. Shortly after midnight on the morning following the recapture, the *Loo* came to a grinding halt. She had struck a reef. Moments later the *Betty* crashed into the same reef. Hopelessly ensnared, the two ships were quickly broken to pieces by the pounding waves. With first light the survivors, huddled in their lifeboats, could see only too clearly the mistake they had made. Out beyond the crushed wreckage of their ships, a line of low, sandy islands stretched toward the horizon. They had blundered into the most deadly navigational obstacle in the Western Hemisphere—the Florida Keys.

The killer reef that ended the days of the *Loo* and the *Betty* is known today as American Shoal and the nearest island as Looe Key. Although the spelling has changed over the years, the key is named for the frigate its reef destroyed. Over the centuries the reef has claimed many other ships as well. Just how many, or even the names of most of the victims, may never be known.

Although the Lighthouse Board had long recommended construction of a light tower at American Shoal, Congress provided no funds for the project until 1878. Built at a shipyard in Trenton, New Jersey, the 109-foot tower was shipped nearly 1,500 miles south to Looe Key, where it was eventually put in place over the shoal. The cost of the station—including the tower, the octagonal keeper's dwelling, which rests on a platform about forty feet above the water, and the first-order Fresnel lens in the lantern room at the top—came to $125,000. Its lamps lit for the first time on July 15, 1880.

The American Shoal Light can still be seen today, nearly 125 years later. The original rotating, bivalve lens was removed when the station was automated in 1963. The modern optic in place today is powered by batteries recharged daily by solar cells.

HOW TO GET THERE:

Near Overseas Highway Mile Marker 17 on Sugarloaf Key, turn left onto Sugarloaf Boulevard (State CR-939) and follow it for 2.4 miles. Then turn right onto State CR-939A and drive 2.5 miles parallel to the beach to a small bridge. The lighthouse can be seen out in the ocean just to the southeast of the bridge.

SAND KEY LIGHT

Southwest of Key West, Florida – 1827 and 1853

In 1820 Joshua Appleby, an out-of-work New England sea captain, migrated from Rhode Island to the Florida Keys in search of a new life. There he became what at the time was commonly known as a "wrecker," one of the freebooting opportunists who salvaged foundered ships and cargoes and sold them for a profit. In the treacherous Keys, where sea traffic was on the increase and unmarked reefs and shoals ripped apart the hulls of ships almost daily, the wrecking business was booming. In the eyes of many, it was a highly questionable enterprise. Seamen often looked upon the wreckers as little better than pirates, and some were, in fact, former buccaneers.

Appleby was no pirate. A hardworking pioneer, he established a thriving settlement on Key Vaca where he fished, turtled, and, when the opportunity came his way, salvaged shipwrecked vessels. The laws about what could be taken and what could not were notoriously vague, and Appleby's perhaps unseemly enthusiasm during an 1823 salvage operation got him thrown into prison. The evidence was thin, however, and Appleby was soon released on orders from President Monroe.

By 1837 the incident had been forgotten. That year Appleby was appointed keeper of the Sand Key Lighthouse, replacing Rebecca Flaherty, who had served as the station's keeper almost since it was established in 1827. A low, almost invisible islet about seven miles to the southwest of Key West, Sand Key had long been a boon to wreckers such as Appleby. Ships regularly ran aground on the island, where they were battered to bits by the waves. Ironically, keeper Appleby now undertook the prevention of just the sort of incidents that had once brought him profits. Every night he faithfully lit the station's fourteen whale-oil lamps and saw to it that the twenty-one-inch, Lewis-style reflector threw its beam far out to sea to give ships ample warning.

A widower, Appleby lived alone on the island except for occasional visits from friends or family. His wrecking career now far in the past, his life was mostly devoid of excitement, except when major squalls or hurricanes struck Sand Key, as they did almost every summer. Appleby and his lighthouse weathered powerful hurricanes in 1841 and again in 1842. Then followed several relatively quiet years.

The summer of 1846 had also been a quiet one, so much so that, when October arrived, the keeper was sure the hurricane season had ended. He felt it safe to invite his daughter Eliza and three-year-old grandson Thomas to the island. With them came Eliza's friend Mary Ann Harris and her adopted daughter. No doubt the visit was a joy for Captain Appleby, but it would end tragically.

On October 9, 1846, Havana was hit by a hurricane so powerful that it left the city in ruins. On the following day that same storm struck the Florida Keys. Appleby and his visitors had no way of knowing what had happened in Cuba or that death was on its way. Likely, it would not have helped if they had known. There was nowhere to run. It is easy to imagine the old seaman checking his barometer every few minutes. The mercury would have dropped so low that he likely thought it was broken. Then the winds and tides came up. By the time they had settled down again on the following day, the light tower and keeper's dwelling were gone. So, too, were Appleby and his visitors—their bodies were never recovered. Sand Key itself had disappeared beneath the waves.

The Sand Key Lighthouse was not rebuilt and returned to service until 1853. Completed under the direction of the recently formed Lighthouse Board and U.S. Army engineer George Meade, the tower was built in what was now open water. Perhaps with the 1846 disaster in mind, Meade gave the tower a solid underfooting of twelve hefty iron pilings. Once complete, the tower stood on twelve heavily braced legs, forming a square with sides sloping inward toward the lantern and gallery at the top. Fitted with a first-order Fresnel lens, it displayed a flashing light capable of warning

HOW TO GET THERE:

The lighthouse can be reached only by boat. Charters are available in nearby Key West. The tower can also be seen and enjoyed from the air. Flying services at the Key West Airport offer tours that include overflights of Sand Key. For information on these and other services, write to the Key West Chamber of Commerce, 402 Wall Street, Key West FL 33040, or call (800) 648–6269.

mariners up to twenty miles away. The grand old Fresnel was removed when the station was automated just before the United States entered World War II in 1941.

Over the years the tower has survived many hurricanes, some of them even stronger than the one that doomed the previous station and its keeper. Unfortunately, the tower was nearly destroyed in a 1989 fire that started in the abandoned keeper's dwelling. The damage was so severe that the Coast Guard had to build a new, temporary light tower some distance from the original one. As of the summer of 1997, a $500,000 restoration project was almost complete.

This spidery 105-foot tower clings to what is left of Sand Key.

KEY WEST LIGHT

Key West, Florida – 1825 and 1847

Florida's greatest menace to shipping is the long chain of low sandy islands and reefs that curve southwestward from Biscayne Bay. Extending more than 200 miles from the mainland, they are known as the Florida Keys, and they rank among the foremost—and most dangerous—navigational obstacles on the planet.

Captains of seventeenth-century Spanish treasure ships called them the *Islas de los Martires,* or Islands of the Martyrs. Some say the islands were given their foreboding name because they were covered with scrubby, wind-twisted trees that reminded Spanish sailors of the tortured bodies of Christian martyrs. Others say the islands earned the name by taking the lives of so many sailors.

Ships met with disaster in the Keys with such regularity that salvaging their cargoes became a lucrative industry, especially following the dramatic increase in commerce that accompanied Florida's acquisition as a U.S. territory. At first American-owned salvage boats, called *wreckers,* worked out of foreign ports, such as Havana, since they had no convenient base in American waters. Likewise, the U.S. Navy had no port to use as a base of operations against the pirates who swarmed through the Keys and the nearby Bahamas. But the Navy located a deep-water harbor at Key West and in 1822 purchased the island from its Spanish owner, Juan Pablo Salas, for $2,000.

Formerly, Key West had been a stronghold for pirates. Now, almost overnight, it grew into a thriving port with a major naval base and large warehouses to store salvaged goods. In 1825 alone almost $300,000 worth of salvage was sold at auction in Key West. That same year the government had a sixty-five-foot lighthouse built on Whitehead Point to mark the entrance to Key West's busy harbor.

Broad verandahs help cool this keeper's residence in steamy Key West. The building houses an excellent maritime museum.

In 1847 the original lighthouse was destroyed—along with much of the town—by a hurricane. The following year a new tower was built. It was located inland of the original lighthouse to protect it from storms and high water. The station received a third-order Fresnel lens in 1872 to replace the original lamp-and-reflector lighting system. The tower was raised by about twenty feet to an overall height of eighty-six feet in 1892. The station was decommissioned in 1969 but restored to active service in 1972 as a private aid to navigation. Today the lighthouse serves as one of many attractions in this sunny, water-besieged tourist mecca.

A $500,000 restoration project in the late 1980s left the Key West Lighthouse in pristine condition.

HOW TO GET THERE:

The Key West Lighthouse and Museum (housed in the station's old keeper's bungalow) are located at the intersection of Truman Avenue (U.S. 1) and Whitehead Street. Opinions differ, of course, but some think this sparkling white tower surrounded by palms is among the most beautiful lighthouses in America. It is certainly one of the most historic. The nearby museum helps visitors grasp the historical significance of both the lighthouse and the town. Among a wide array of fascinating exhibits is a fourth-order Fresnel bull's-eye lens. For more information contact the Key West Lighthouse Museum, 938 Whitehead Street, Key West, FL 33040; (305) 294–0012. For other tourist information contact the Key West Chamber of Commerce, 402 Wall Street, Key West, FL 33040; (305) 294–2587 or (800) 648–6269.

GARDEN KEY LIGHT

Dry Tortugas, Florida – 1826 and 1876

About 120 miles west-southwest of the Florida peninsula, a scattering of small islands and reefs rise out of the Gulf of Mexico. These are the Dry Tortugas, the final link in the long chain of the Florida Keys. Here warm waters of the Gulf meet the cooler waters of the Atlantic, creating a navigator's nightmare of swirls and eddies. These unpredictable currents combine with a jumble of ship-killing shoals and shallows to make this one of the most dangerous places in all the world's oceans.

The Tortugas lie directly astride the vital shipping lanes linking ports on the Gulf with those on the East Coast. By acquiring Florida from the Spanish in 1821, the United States hoped to secure this all-important trade route. No sooner had Florida become U.S. territory than the Navy was sent to flush pirates out of the Keys. Then, to protect ships from natural obstacles—far more numerous than pirates—along the route, the government began to mark threatening islands, reefs, and headlands with lights and other navigational aids. The process was to be expensive and time consuming. More than half a century would pass before an adequate system was finally in place.

Among the first sites chosen for a major light was Garden Key in the Dry Tortugas. Funded by an appropriation of less than $11,000, the project was started early in 1824, but it took more than two years to complete. Things got off to a very poor start when a ship carrying the materials and supplies to the remote key was lost without at trace at sea. Destructive squalls further slowed construction, so

The black Garden Key tower is now Fort Jefferson's lone sentinel. (Photo courtesy Florida Department of Commerce Division of Tourism)

that the seventy-foot conical brick tower was not ready for service until the summer of 1826. Keeper John Flaherty, who, along with his life Rebecca, would later keep the light at Sand Key, first lighted the Garden Key lamps on the night of July 4, 1826.

The strategic significance of the Tortugas was not lost on U.S. military officials. It was believed that a foreign armed force occupying one or more of the small islands here could easily block the economically vital Gulf shipping lanes. To guard against this, the U.S. Army began construction of a mighty fort on Garden Key in 1846. Although work on Fort Jefferson continued for almost thirty years, it was never completed. Even so, it is an impressive structure, with walls fifty-five feet high and eight feet thick and containing more than forty million bricks. Sometimes called the "Gibraltar of the Gulf," Fort Jefferson's garrison could house up to 1,500 troops, and its 450 smooth-bore cannon were capable of pummeling an entire enemy fleet. One of its enormous artillery pieces fired cannonballs weighing half a ton. Needless to say, anything hit by these hefty projectiles would have been seriously damaged. Ironically, the fort's cannon never fired a shot in anger.

Completely surrounded by shark-infested waters, Fort Jefferson was used mostly as a prison. During the Civil War captured Confederates were held here, but the fort's most famous prisoner was not a soldier. Following the assassination of President Abraham Lincoln, a vengeful court convicted Maryland physician Samuel Mudd of treason for having set the broken leg of John Wilkes Booth. Although Dr. Mudd played no role in the crime itself and had no idea Booth was an assassin, he nonetheless found himself chained in a stinking cell at Fort Jefferson.

The bewildered and—nearly everyone now agrees—innocent Dr. Mudd had sweltered in his cell for nearly two years by late 1867 when a yellow-fever epidemic struck Garden Key. Undeterred by the supposed threat of exposure to the disease (which we now know is spread mostly by mosquitoes), the doctor volunteered to assist the victims. For his humanitarian efforts, he was pardoned in 1869.

For many years the original Garden Key Lighthouse stood on the parade ground of Fort Jefferson, its lantern room barely peeking over the high walls of the fort. After a hurricane severely damaged the tower in 1873, a new one was built on top of the walls. A thirty-seven-foot-tall cast-iron structure, it was completed and placed in service on April 5, 1876. Its fourth-order Fresnel lens, illuminated by kerosene lamps, gave the beacon a range of approximately sixteen miles. The light was decommissioned in 1912.

HOW TO GET THERE:

Garden Key and its lighthouse are now part of Dry Tortugas National Park, which encompasses nearly 65,000 acres of coral reef and churning surf, but only forty acres of dry land. In addition to the lighthouses at Garden Key and Loggerhead Key, attractions include historic Fort Jefferson and a one-hundred-square-mile naturalist's paradise where ocean mammals, sharks, fish, and seabirds of every variety abound.

The Tortugas are not just a long way from the mainland; they are 70 miles from Key West, the remote terminus of the Overseas Highway. The only way to reach them is by sea or air. Charter boats, ferries, and scheduled seaplane service are available from Key West. For listings, schedules, and fees, contact the Key West Chamber of Commerce, 402 Wall Street, Key West, FL 33040; (800) 648–6269. For park information contact Dry Tortugas National Park, P.O. Box 6208, Key West, FL 33041.

DRY TORTUGAS LIGHT

Loggerhead Key, Florida – 1858

ew navigational obstacles are as threatening to seamen as the Dry Tortugas, where nearly a hundred square miles of reef lurk just below the ocean's surface. Recognizing the danger these vast shoals posed to shipping, the U.S. government placed one of Florida's earliest lighthouses on Garden Key near the middle of the Tortugas island chain. Almost from the moment it entered service in 1826, however, seamen complained that the light was difficult to see. Meanwhile, shipwrecks in the Tortugas continued with alarming regularity. The captains of some ruined vessels claimed they could not see the light at all until it was too late to change course and avoid disaster.

Maritime officials agreed that a new and better light was needed to mark the Tortugas, but nothing would be done to improve the situation for almost two decades. Under the tightfisted tutelage of Treasury Department auditor Stephen Pleasonton, the Lighthouse Service of that era rarely if ever opted to fund a new facility when one was already in place—no matter how poorly it functioned. Only after Pleasonton was at long last forced into retirement during the 1850s was a second Tortugas lighthouse finally built.

Funded by a congressional appropriation of $35,000, the new 157-foot tower was completed in 1858. Located on Loggerhead Key, it stood a reasonably safe distance from Garden Key, where the thunder of Fort Jefferson's massive guns often shattered lantern windows and periodic outbreaks of yellow fever threatened keepers and their families. The tower's height and state-of-the-art second-order Fresnel lens gave the beacon a range of more than twenty miles. This provided watchful seamen with plenty of warning and time to steer around the Tortugas.

Severely damaged by a hurricane in 1873, the tower was at first thought to be a complete loss. However, the masons sent to do emergency repairs managed to save the structure. In fact, they did their work so well that the tower still stands today, having survived at least a dozen additional major hurricanes.

Because of its remote location, the station's full-time crew was removed in 1925 and an automatic acetylene lamp placed on the lantern. In 1986 the original clamshell Fresnel lens was replaced by a modern optic that could be more easily maintained. Nonetheless, the Dry Tortugas beacon, flashing white every twenty seconds, is still closely watched by seamen anxious to avoid the Tortugas reefs.

(Photo by Bob and Sandra Shanklin)

HOW TO GET THERE:

oggerhead Key and its lighthouse are located within the 65,000-acre confines of Dry Tortugas National Park. For information on charter boats, ferries, and seaplanes providing access to the park, contact the Key West Chamber of Commerce, 402 Wall Street, Key West, FL 33040; (800) 648–6269. For information on the park, its abundant wildlife, and historic attractions such as Fort Jefferson, contact Dry Tortugas National Park, P.O. Box 6208, Key West, FL 33041.

CHAPTER TWO

Lights of
THE TREASURE SANDS
FLORIDA WEST COAST *and* PANHANDLE

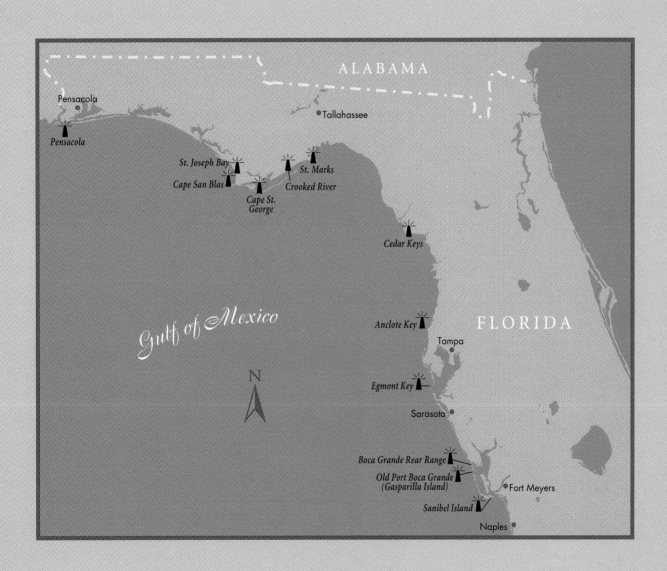

ALABAMA

Pensacola

Pensacola

• Tallahassee

St. Joseph Bay

Cape San Blas

St. Marks

Crooked River

Cape St.
George

Cedar Keys

Gulf of Mexico

Anclote Key

FLORIDA

Tampa

N

Egmont Key

Sarasota

Boca Grande Rear Range

Old Port Boca Grande
(Gasparilla Island)

Fort Meyers

Sanibel Island

Naples

In this remote corner of the Florida Panhandle, the St. Marks Lighthouse guards the border between land and sea.

By the mid-1800s the United States had more lighthouses than any other nation on earth. More than 200 major or minor lights shined from one place or another along its coasts. But while America's light towers outnumbered those of other maritime powers such as Britain, France, or Spain, they lagged far behind in the quality of their construction and the reliability of their beacons. Improvements, such as the use of the advanced, though expensive, Fresnel lenses, were delayed by the tight budgets imposed by Congress and by the bureaucratic monovision of treasury auditor Stephen Pleasonton. For more than thirty years, beginning in 1820, Pleasonton lorded over the Lighthouse Service like an oriental satrap—and a parsimonious one at that. By 1850, however, Pleasonton's influence began to wane, unleashing a revolution in American lighthouse technology.

In 1852 a Lighthouse Board composed of experienced military officers, engineers, and seamen took charge of the Service. Almost immediately the Board embarked on an ambitious program aimed at expanding and upgrading navigational aids along all of America's coasts. With the U.S. economy booming and coastal trade on the increase, Congress was willing to foot the huge bill for these improvements.

Not surprisingly, the Board focused special attention on marking the Florida Keys and the shores of the Gulf of Mexico. The most vulnerable stretch of the liquid highway used to transport the abundant produce of the midwest to population centers in the east, the Gulf was vital to the nation's economic survival. Ironically, its shoal- and reef-strewn coast was poorly marked. To deal with this problem, the Board would rely on the skills, energy, and fresh ideas of young military engineers such as George Gordon Meade and Danville Leadbetter.

A SEA CAPTAIN'S LAMP

Winslow Lewis had epitomized the old way of building lighthouses. A former New England sea captain, he represented the age of wooden sailing ships, stone forts, and, naturally enough, stone light towers. About 1810, while suffering through a long stretch of unemployment, Lewis invented a lamp-and-parabolic-reflector system that he said would make America's navigational beacons more powerful. The Lewis system was quickly adopted, and the U.S. government paid him $60,000 to place his devices in all of the nation's lighthouses, a process that would take him seven years. No doubt, Lewis's reflectors were a considerable improvement over earlier systems, but they would prove vastly inferior to the Fresnel lens soon developed by the French. Even so, the Lighthouse Service would keep most of its Lewis reflectors in place until after 1850.

Having found an advocate in Pleasonton, who admired his knack for thrift, Lewis was soon being hired not just to equip lighthouses but to build them. He preferred towers of a conventional, conical design with stout walls of stone or brick, and he built them well. Many of the dozens of light towers Lewis built on sites from Maine to Louisiana still stand. Among the Gulf Coast lighthouses built by Lewis were those at St. Marks, Cape St. George, and St. Joseph Bay.

Perhaps Lewis's best-known success—and failure—came at Frank's Island, Louisiana, where he was hired in 1818 to build an ornate lighthouse and customs office near the primary entrance to the Mississippi. Designed by a government architect who had never visited the site, the absurdly inappropriate structure was far too heavy for the river's delta marshlands and collapsed into a pile of useless rubble only a few days after it was finished. Lewis then contracted to build a sensibly modest tower of his own design, completing it, as we would say nowadays, under budget and ahead of schedule. Although the tower has sunk more than twenty feet into the Mississippi mud, it still stands, a testament to the workmanship of Lewis's construction crews. But Lewis's outmoded reflectors and stone towers were no match for the challenges that would face the Lighthouse Service in the 1850s.

TWO LIGHTHOUSE GENERALS

George Meade could hardly have presented a sharper contrast to Winslow Lewis. Part of a younger, better-educated generation of American lighthouse experts, Meade was a trained engineer. In 1835 Meade graduated from West Point at the age of only twenty. After fighting in the Seminole War in Florida, he became a surveyor for the Army Corps of Topographical Engineers, helping to set the boundary between the United States and the then Republic of Texas. In time he developed an interest in marine engineering and lighthouses. His innovative work on light towers in the Delaware Bay convinced his superiors that Lieutenant

Meade could help with the seemingly impossible task of marking the Florida Keys.

Arriving at Carysfort Reef in 1850, Meade supervised construction of an iron-skeleton lighthouse designed by I.W.P. Lewis, who happened to be the nephew—and harshest critic—of Winslow Lewis. The revolutionary screw-pile technology and open structure of the Carysfort tower appealed to the modern instincts of Meade the engineer. It was an approach Meade would take—and improve on—again and again over the next several years as he built towers at Sand Key, Sombrero Key, and Rebecca Shoal. One essential Meade innovation was the use of large metal discs to help anchor screw piles to an unstable sand or coral base. Of course, Meade always sought to match methods to the designs of the site. For Seahorse Key, located well to the north of Tampa and off the track followed by most hurricanes, he designed a classic brick-and-wood-frame combination tower and dwelling much like those later built in the northwest.

Another U.S. Army engineer building Gulf lighthouses at about this time was Captain Danville Leadbetter. Although a few years older than Meade, Leadbetter had graduated from West Point one year later, in 1836.

Instead of iron and steel, Leadbetter preferred to use brick, but his often octagonal towers proved as

A victim of recent Gulf storms, the Cape St. George tower leans precariously toward the sea. Efforts are underway to save it.

stable and durable as any of the skeleton structures built by Meade. Completed in 1858, his tower at Sand Island off Alabama's Mobile stood more than 200 feet tall. Leadbetter's brick tower at Port Pontchartrain was stabilized by a submerged concrete pad. His most unusual design may have been that of the Sabine Pass Lighthouse, with its extraordinary finlike buttresses. Spreading the weight of the tower over the damp, yielding ground, the buttresses have held the tower in rock-solid plumb for more than 140 years. A Leadbetter design for the Cape San Blas Lighthouse in the Florida Panhandle region was never built but might have been a wonder to behold. His creative plan called for a ninety-foot brick tower set atop screw-pile stilts.

THE ARCHITECTURE OF VICTORY

The outbreak of the Civil War in 1861 changed the professional status and destiny of millions. Among these millions were Meade, who quickly rose to the rank of general in the Union Army, and Leadbetter, who did the same on the Confederate side. But the war had very different fates in store for the two men.

Highly valued for his engineering skills, General Leadbetter was put in charge of Gulf Coast fortifications and, not coincidentally, its lighthouses. With a navy vastly inferior to that of the Union, however, the Confederates had little use for coastal lights, likely to benefit only their enemies. Under Leadbetter's direction, Southern troops often removed and carefully hid Fresnel lenses and other useful equipment to keep them out of the hands of the enemy. But some lighthouses thought to be of particular use to Union blockade fleets were marked for destruction. In a moment of supreme and poignant irony, Leadbetter sent out a raiding party to blow up the Sand Island Lighthouse, which he himself had so proudly built only a few years earlier.

As the war progressed and began to go badly for the South, Leadbetter was recruited to design defensive positions for Confederate infantry. As it turned out, the general had far less skill in creating structures meant to take lives than he had had earlier with light towers intended to save them. His entrenchments and other defensive arrangements were thought by some to have been partly responsible for Confederate defeats at Knoxville and Chattanooga.

Following the war there were few opportunities in the United States for a former Confederate general to work as a lighthouse engineer. To support himself and

Robert E. Lee surveyed a site for the Egmont Key Lighthouse in the late 1840s. Union forces kept Confederate prisoners here during the Civil War. (Courtesy U.S. Coast Guard)

his family, Leadbetter sought work in Mexico and Canada. Exhausted, he died in Canada in 1866, little more than a year after he returned to civilian life.

Meade, on the other hand, fought in several important engagements while working his way up to the rank of major general. A string of early defeats suffered by the Union Army of the Potomac had led President Lincoln to fire one general after another. Meade inherited this revolving-door command on the eve of the critical battle of Gettysburg. Had Robert E. Lee's Confederates won this battle and surged on toward Washington, the South would likely have won the war. But Meade had learned in Florida how to build a structure capable of weathering a storm. On a series of hills overlooking Gettysburg, he erected his defense, and on the third and final day of the battle, when Lee let loose the 13,000-man hurricane of Pickett's charge, its foundations held fast.

Innovative lighthouse engineers George Meade (left) and Danville Leadbetter (right) fought on opposite sides during the Civil War. Meade led the Union to victory at Gettysburg, while Leadbetter was far less successful as a designer of Confederate entrenchments. (Left: Photo courtesy Massachusetts Commandery Military Order of the Loyal Legion of the U.S. Army Military History Institute. Right: Drawing from Harpers Weekly from private collection of Jim Claflin.)

SANIBEL ISLAND LIGHT

Sanibel Island, Florida – 1884

During the 1920s auto maker Henry Ford and his old friend Thomas Edison came to Florida's Fort Myers each year to escape the long northern winter. The two shared an occasional ferry outing to lush Sanibel Island, located a few miles off the mainland. No doubt, when they made the crossing during the evening, their eyes caught the flash of the Sanibel Island Lighthouse on Point Ybel. Ironically, the light they saw was not produced by one of Mr. Edison's lightbulbs. Instead, it came from a kerosene lamp. (Somewhat later the station would employ an acetylene lamp.) The lighthouse did not receive an electric lamp until 1962—by which time Ford and Edison had long since passed from the scene—making it one of the last light stations in America to be electrified.

Time—and what nonislanders like to call progress—often move slowly on extraordinarily beautiful Sanibel. The lighthouse itself was a very long time coming. By 1833 early island settlers and local fishermen were already petitioning Congress for a light. Their pleas fell on deaf ears, however, until the 1850s, when the newly formed Lighthouse Board recommended that a light station be placed here. Still nothing was done, and Congress appropriated no money for the project until 1883, a full half century after the first petitions were submitted.

With $50,000 in federal money available for the project, a supply ship carrying iron for the station's tower set sail from New Jersey bound for Sanibel. Only a few miles short of the island, it struck a shoal and sank. Salvagers from Key West managed to pull most of the materials off the sandy sea bottom, and at long last, construction of the tower got underway. The station's lamps were officially lit on August 20, 1884.

An iron-skeleton–style structure, designed to withstand hurricane winds, the tower stands on four legs braced by girds and tie bars. A central metal-walled cylinder provides access to the lantern via a winding staircase of 127 steps. Soaring one-hundred feet above the low, sandy point, the lantern room once housed a third-order Fres-

nel lens, displaying a flashing white beacon. The light guided ships past the point and into the nearby deepwater port of Punta Rassa. The old French-made glass lens was replaced with a modern plastic lens some years ago when the station was automated. However, the light remains active to this day.

The tower is listed on the National Register of Historic Places. So, too, are the adjacent tropical-style keeper's cottages. Built on piles, the cottages have steeply sloped pyramidal roofs and are wrapped around by wide verandahs.

HOW TO GET THERE:

The station can be reached from Fort Myers via the Sanibel Causeway, Highway 867, and Lighthouse Road. The tower and other buildings are closed to the public, but visitors may walk the station grounds. The area around the lighthouse is part of the J. N. "Ding" Darling National Wildlife Refuge. The refuge visitors' center is located at One Wildlife Road just off San-Cap Road. For information on Sanibel, the refuge, and attractions in the Fort Myers area, call (800) 533–4753.

(Photo by Bob and Sandra Shanklin)

BOCA GRANDE REAR RANGE LIGHT

Boca Grande, Florida – 1932

In the sixteenth century and again in the seventeenth, the gold-hungry and ever-optimistic Spanish tramped Florida from end to end searching for the glittering yellow metal. They found none. During the late nineteenth century, however, Florida became the center of a mining bonanza; its focus was not gold or silver, however, but phosphate. Vast deposits of this acidic mineral, used to make chemical fertilizers, were discovered beneath the state's southern marshlands. By the turn of the twentieth century, enormous quantities of phosphate were moving through the small town of Boca Grande on Gasparilla Island.

The phosphate arrived at Boca Grande by rail, then was shipped by freighter through the Gulf of Mexico to chemical plants along the Mississippi. In 1932 a range-light system was established to guide the chemical freighters in and out of the harbor. The term *range light* refers to twin lights, the first placed above and to the rear of the second. When a navigator sees the lights stacked one atop the other, he knows his ship is in midchannel. If the upper of the two lights appears to tilt either to the right or left, the vessel is drifting out of the safe channel in the direction indicated. The Boca Grande Rear Range Light was intended to function in just this way in concert with the older Gasparilla Island Lighthouse, located about a mile away in Port Boca Grande.

Usually, the rear range beacon is the more substantial of the two. The front range light may be mounted on a pole or jetty, while its rear range sister light is usually a more tradition lighthouse tower. Here the front range light is provided by an older, established lighthouse, while the rear range light consists of a steel-skeleton tower rising more than 105 feet above the water. With its peaked metal roof, the gangly tower is slightly suggestive of the tinman in *The Wizard of Oz.*

The tower's light, produced by an aeromarine optic, remains in service. Over the years it has become less and less useful to seamen, however. Development of Boca Grande's valuable shorefront property has placed so many bright lights in competition with the old beacon that navigators now find it quite difficult to distinguish among them.

HOW TO GET THERE:

There are two lighthouses on this scenic Gulf Coast island. This one is located just south of the town of Boca Grande. The other is about 2 miles to the south in the Gasparilla Island Recreation Area (see previous section on Old Port Boca Grande Light). To reach Gasparilla Island from U.S. Highway 41, follow State 776 and State 771 to Placida. Then follow signs to the Boca Grande Causeway and toll bridge leading to Gasparilla Island. The rear range lighthouse stands just off Gulf Boulevard beside Boca Grande Beach. This little public beach offers some of the best fishing and shelling anywhere on the Gulf of Mexico. It is also a wonderful spot for a late-afternoon picnic. Try not to miss the sunset.

OLD PORT BOCA GRANDE (GASPARILLA ISLAND) LIGHT

Gasparilla Island, Florida – 1890

Built in 1890 on Gasparilla Island, Old Port Boca Grande Lighthouse lights the southern stretches of the Florida coast and, some say, marks the grave of a headless Spanish princess. The island is named for José Gaspar, a bloodthirsty pirate with a lusty appetite for gold, silver, and beautiful women. Gaspar's raids on merchant ships netted him many female prisoners, whom he kept on Gasparilla, which he called *Cautiva*, meaning "captive woman."

One of Gaspar's captives, a beautiful Spanish princess named Josefa, turned the tables on the pirate by imprisoning his heart. Gaspar was so stricken with the lady that he begged her to marry him. However, the proud Josefa answered his marriage plea with a curse and spat in his eye. In a fit of rage, the pirate drew his saber and beheaded her. Overwhelmed with remorse, Gaspar buried Josefa's body on the beach where he had murdered her. To remind him of his love for the princess, he kept her head in a jar on his ship. It is said that Josefa's decapitated ghost still walks the island in search of its missing head.

Boca Grande Lighthouse sits on iron stilts above the erosive surf near the mouth of Charlotte Harbor. The lighthouse was abandoned by the U.S. Coast Guard in 1967 and quickly became prey for vandals and the elements. In an effort to preserve it, local residents had the lighthouse transferred from federal to local ownership in 1972. In 1980 it was placed on the National Register of Historic Places.

The Gasparilla Island Conservation and Improvement Association began restoring Boca Grande Light in late 1985, with grants from the Bureau of Historic Preservation, the Florida Department of State, and the Historic Preservation Advisory Council. As part of this effort, the Coast Guard reinstalled Boca Grande's crown—the original imported French Fresnel lens—and on November 21, 1986, the old lighthouse was ceremoniously relit for active federal service to navigation.

Erosion has long plagued Gasparilla Island. Since 1950 the ocean has gobbled up more than a million square feet of shorefront property, lopping off nearly a quarter of a mile from the southern end of the island. By 1970 seawater was lapping at the supports that hold up the lighthouse. Local residents and preservationists asked for federal help, but their pleas at first fell on deaf ears. Only after the eroded soil began to fill the nearby channel with sandbars and threaten shipping did the government act.

In 1971 a 265-foot granite jetty was built to resist the clawing Gulf currents. Then local companies dumped more 100,000 cubic yards of fill into the shallows, much of it in front of the old lighthouse. Apparently, the old station has been saved to be enjoyed by future generations of lighthouse lovers.

HOW TO GET THERE:

The lighthouse is located in Gasparilla Island State Recreation Area at the far southern tip of the island. From U.S. Highway 41 follow State 776 and State 771 to Placida. Then follow signs to the Boca Grande Causeway and toll bridge leading to Gasparilla Island. Port Boca Grande and the lighthouse are located at the far end of Gulf Boulevard. In addition to the lighthouse, the recreation area offers picnicking, fishing, shelling, and glorious ocean views. For more information contact Gasparilla Island Recreation Area, P.O. Box 1150, Boca Grande, FL 33921.

EGMONT KEY LIGHT

St. Petersburg – 1848 and 1858

ernando DeSoto may have been the first European to set foot on the small, sandy island known today as Egmont Key. Some believe that DeSoto pitched camp on the island in 1539, before launching his famous exploration of the North American interior—a trek that would take him all the way to the Mississippi River. But it was the British who gave the key its unusual name, almost two centuries later, when a royal survey team charted the Gulf Coast. The name honors the Earl of Egmont, who was at that time Lord of the Admiralty. One might wonder why the earl rated so small an honor—why, for instance, his surveyors had not attached his name to

(Photo by Bob and Sandra Shanklin)

the impressive bay behind the little island or to the vast peninsula beyond. The answer, of course, is that the Spanish had long ago given names to those particular natural features. They were called Tampa Bay and Florida.

After Florida became part of the United States in 1821, Tampa Bay emerged as an important trading center, and its commercial vitality steadily increased. By the 1830s Florida settlers were asking the federal government to mark the bay with a lighthouse, but no action was taken for nearly two decades. A lighthouse was finally built on Egmont Key in 1848 by contractor Francis Gibbons for $10,000. Despite a five-month delay due to a lack of bricks—none could be found for sale along the entire coast of western Florida—the contractor had the tower and a small keeper's dwelling standing in just over half a year. Having earned a reputation at Egmont Key for solid workmanship, Gibbons was later hired to build the first lighthouses on the coasts of California, Oregon, and Washington State.

The same year Gibbons completed its lighthouse, Egmont Key was visited by an Army surveyor with the rather famous name of Robert E. Lee. Although Lee thought the strategically located island an ideal location for a stone fort, none was ever built there. However, the brick walls of the new forty-foot-high light tower at the north end of the island soon earned a reputation for being as strong as a fortress.

During the autumn of its first year of operation, the station was struck by a strong Gulf hurricane. Keeper Sherrod Edwards and his family only managed to save themselves by climbing into a small boat and riding out the fifteen-foot tide that swept over the island. A few weeks later a second hurricane hit Egmont Key, and after it had passed, the storm-weary Edwards took his family and left the island, never to return. Luckily for the station and the seamen who depended on it for guidance, later keepers proved hardier and less easily discouraged.

The storms kept coming, year after year, and while their winds never quite managed to topple the tower, flooding tides did eventually undermine it. In 1858 the original Gibbons lighthouse had to be torn down and rebuilt. Masons reinforced the new eighty-seven-foot masonry tower with walls more than three feet thick. Those stout, brick walls have since stood up to more than 140 years of hurricanes and gales. Located at the north end of the island, the structure still stands, and its automated light remains active.

Early in the Civil War, an overwhelming Union force swept away a small Confederate garrison on Egmont Key. Afterwards the Union side used the island as a base for raids on Confederate coastal defenses. Later the island became a prison for captured Southern sailors and soldiers. Many fighting men, both Union and Confederate, died of wounds and disease at the prison hospital. Their bodies lay buried in a small cemetery on the key until 1909, when they were disinterred and moved to cemeteries on the mainland.

HOW TO GET THERE:

Egmont Key and its lighthouse can be reached only by boat. Charters and rentals are available at several marinas in the Tampa Bay area. Boaters should note that the island offers no public docks, but small craft can be anchored just off shore. The tower and its light can be seen and enjoyed from nearby Fort De Soto State Park as well. To reach the park, follow Routes 682 and 679 south from St. Petersburg. For more information call the St. Petersburg Visitors Bureau at (813) 464–7200 or contact the Greater Tampa Chamber of Commerce, Tampa, FL 33601–0420; (813) 228–7777.

ANCLOTE KEY LIGHT

Tarpon Springs, Florida – 1887

Anclote Key, a long, thin Gulf island just to the west of Tarpon Springs, Florida, has always been popular with insects. People, on the other hand, often find the place somewhat less inviting. For many years the keepers of the Anclote Key Lighthouse were the island's only human inhabitants and, constantly under assault by clouds of hungry mosquitoes, even they were not always glad to be there.

For a brief period in 1682, however, Anclote Key was one of the busiest spots in Florida. Early that year an entire fleet of pirate ships anchored here, and more than 400 buccaneers went ashore to sharpen their cutlasses and ready themselves for raids along the nearby coast. Using the island as a base, this lawless armada attacked and devastated dozens of small, defenseless mainland settlements. Then, a few months after they had arrived, the pirates moved on to overwhelm the Spanish Fort at San Marcos.

More than two centuries would pass before the island was invaded again, this time by construction workers hired in 1887 to build the Anclote Key Lighthouse. Like the earlier invasion, this one would be brief. Prefabricated in a northern shipyard, the ninety-six-foot, steel-skeleton tower was bolted together quickly. Begun in June, the station was completed and ready for service within two months. Keeper James Gardner lit the kerosene lamps inside its third-order Fresnel lens on September 15, 1887. Flashing red every thirty seconds, the beacon could be distinguished easily from that of the fixed white light on nearby Egmont Key.

The Anclote Key keepers and their families, who often lived with them on the island, suffered through the same powerful storms and flood tides that plagued other Gulf Coast light stations. Hurricanes often curl up through the Gulf to strike the western coast of Florida. But the keepers' worst—and certainly most annoying—problem was the island's prodigious population of mosquitoes. Drainage canals, dug by Depression-era WPA workers in hopes of controlling these droning pests, did little to keep them down. No doubt it was with a sense of relief that the last keepers left the island when the Coast Guard discontinued the light in 1952.

Although abandoned nearly half a century ago, the old tower still stands. The dwelling and other station buildings, however, were long ago removed. Today the tower is part of the Anclote National Wildlife Refuge.

(Photo by Bob and Sandra Shanklin)

HOW TO GET THERE:

Located a little less than 3 miles from the mainland, Anclote Key is easily accessible to boaters. The lighthouse stands at the south end of the island, which is now protected as the Anclote National Wildlife Refuge. The island's beaches are especially beautiful. Island Wind Tours offers excursions to the island and lighthouse; call (813) 934–0606. For more information contact the Tarpon Springs Chamber of Commerce at 11 East Orange Street, Tarpon Springs, FL 34689; (813) 937–6109.

CEDAR KEYS LIGHT

Seahorse Key, Florida – 1854

It is said by some in Florida that the Suwannee River is so crooked that anyone crossing it will end up back where he started. The winding waterway immortalized by Stephan Foster's classic lyric, "Way Down Upon the Suwannee River," finally wriggles and twists its way into the Gulf of Mexico a dozen miles or so to the north of a small island chain known as the Cedar Keys. Covered in scrubby forests, these islands were formed long ago from eroded soils washed into the Gulf by the Suwannee and the equally snakelike Waccasassa River some miles to the south.

During the mid-eighteenth century, pencil manufacturers discovered an ideal use for the namesake cedars that grew in clutches all over the keys. Students and teachers throughout the country were soon equipped with writing implements made with dense Cedar Keys hardwood. The hunger for cedar and other fine woods that grew in abundance here attracted a steady parade of lumber ships. To guide them and to warn mariners against the navigational threat posed by the islands, the government established a light station in 1854.

Built under the watchful eye of U.S. Army engineer George Meade, later a Civil War general, the lighthouse was placed on Seahorse Key, about 3 miles southwest of Cedar Key, the largest island in the chain. Meade had supervised construction of several other important Florida lighthouses, including those at Carysfort Reef, Sombrero Key, and Sand Key. All of the towers Meade built in the lower Florida Keys were of the iron-skeleton type, a design intended to protect them from hurricane winds. Seahorse Key, however, lay hundreds of miles to the north of Meade's earlier lighthouses and in an area supposedly less prone to hurricanes. The inexpensive structure he built here consisted of a one-story brick dwelling with a squat tower perched on its roof. The entire project was completed at a cost to the government of only $12,000—a bargain-basement price considering that construction of the Sombrero Key Lighthouse had tapped the U.S. Treasury for a whopping $150,000.

Although the little Cedar Keys Lighthouse was only twenty-eight-feet high, it stood on a hill, placing the focal plane of its beacon some seventy-five feet above the water. Its fourth-order Fresnel lens produced a fixed white light visible from fifteen miles away.

At the beginning of the Civil War, Confederate officials had the lens and supplies of whale oil removed from the station. For several months Seahorse Key was guarded by a small garrison of Southern troops, but they were soon captured by a Union gunboat. Although it remained dark throughout the war, the lighthouse returned to active service in 1866.

During the last years of the nineteenth century, the economy of the Cedar Key area fell on hard times. The most valuable timber had already been cut, and local commercial fishing grounds and oyster beds began to play out. Fewer and fewer freighters steamed into the port of Cedar Key. With traffic slowed to a mere trickle, the Cedar Keys Lighthouse was permanently darkened in 1915. Today Seahorse Key is part of a wildlife refuge.

HOW TO GET THERE:

Located in an environmentally sensitive wildlife refuge, Seahorse Key is closed to the public. University students live at the old light station while doing research on the island. The station and refuge can be seen from the water, however. For information on boats and excursions, contact the Cedar Key Chamber of Commerce, P.O. Box 610, Cedar Key, FL 32625; (904) 543–5600. Known for its great fishing and seafood, the Cedar Keys area is well worth a visit. The town of Cedar Key can be reached from U.S. Highway 19 or I–75 by following State 24 South.

(Photo by Bob and Sandra Shanklin)

ST. MARKS LIGHT

St. Marks, Florida – 1831

Florida history buffs like to argue that the first lighthouse in North America stood on the banks of the St. Marks River near the point where their state begins to bend westward into its panhandle. They make the rather intriguing assertion that the Spanish, during their early explorations, raised a light at the mouth of the river. But like those who claim priority for the French light at The Balize in Louisiana, they can cite no decisive evidence; the Boston Harbor Light, built in 1716, remains generally recognized as America's first lighthouse.

The old Spanish light, if it ever existed at all, was gone by the early eighteenth century, when control of the area passed from Spain to the United States. But officials in Washington soon recognized the commercial importance of the Spanish settlement at St. Marks, and in 1828 Congress appropriated $6,000 for a light to mark the entrance of the harbor. The builders must have been the ancestors of some of today's government contractors; they scrimped on materials to such an extent that the walls were actually left hollow. In fact, their work was so shoddy that the tower had to be demolished, lest it fall down of its own accord and hurt somebody.

The new, solid-walled tower erected in its place was well constructed, but the masons who built it might as well have saved themselves the sweat. The river quickly undercut its foundations, forcing the government to pull

Despite Confederate attempts to blow up the St. Marks Light during the Civil War, the light was restored and remains a landmark today.

it down yet again and rebuild it on another, safer location.

This third tower was truly a fine piece of work and raised the lantern to a point seventy-three feet above sea level. From this height its fifteen lamps and fifteen-inch reflectors enabled it to be seen by ships more than a dozen miles at sea. The brick-and-mortar tower still stands, despite the violence to which nature and man have subjected it.

During the Seminole Indian Wars, a nervous keeper pleaded for an army detachment to protect the light station—and his scalp. His superiors ignored him and, luckily, so did the rebellious Seminoles. But when the Civil War broke out, the rebels in gray did not ignore the lighthouse. Fearing it would be used to guide Union ships into the strategic St. Marks Harbor, Confederate soldiers tried to blow it up with kegs of gunpowder stacked inside the tower. The blast knocked out a full third of its circumference, but the stubborn tower put on a superb balancing act and refused to fall. Shortly after the war the Lighthouse Board managed to repair the lighthouse and, by early 1867, had it back in service.

The St. Marks Lighthouse still lights each night and remains among the most picturesque sights on the Gulf Coast. Located in a pristine refuge, alive with seabirds and other wildlife, it is well worth a visit.

HOW TO GET THERE:

Located in the St. Marks National Wildlife Refuge, the lighthouse can be reached by taking State 363 from Tallahassee to St. Marks. Follow signs to the wildlife refuge and take County Road 59 to the lighthouse. The large parking area serves birdwatchers, beach users, and lighthouse visitors.

The tower and keeper's house are open to the public only once a year, sometime in mid-May; group tours can be arranged by writing to Officer in Charge, USCG ANT, Thomas Drive, Panama City, Florida 32407–5898. It is well worth the trip to see this lighthouse, probably the most photographed lighthouse on the Gulf Coast. Birds and alligators abound in the swamps surrounding the lighthouse. Bring your camera.

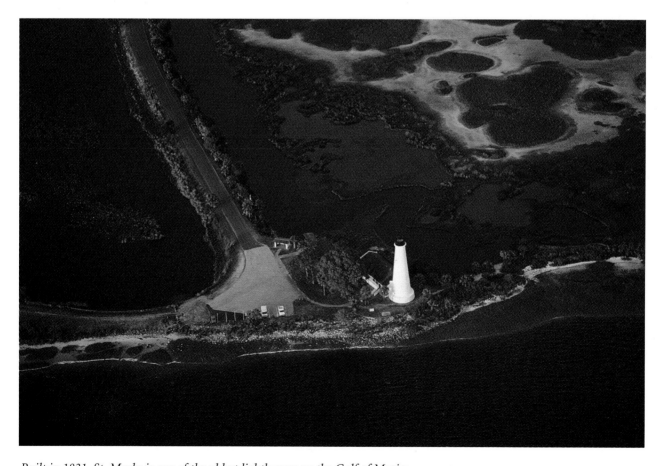

Built in 1831, St. Marks is one of the oldest lighthouses on the Gulf of Mexico.

CROOKED RIVER LIGHT

Carrrabelle, Florida – 1895

As early as 1838 a small, isolated light station operated on windy Dog Island, a few miles south of Carrabelle, Florida. For decades lights there guided freighters into the mouth of the aptly named Crooked River, where they took on valuable loads of hardwood lumber. Then, one day in the fall of 1873, the station keeper looked out into the gulf and saw a mass of black clouds rushing at him from the south. This was no mere gale but a hurricane packing killer winds and a flood tide that soon put the entire island under water. The storm swept the low, sandy island clean, dumping the lighthouse, the keeper's dwelling, and, probably, the keeper himself into the sea. Following this disaster the board decided not to rebuild the Dog Island Lighthouse.

Lumber boats and freighters, however, continued to pay frequent visits to Carrabelle. By the 1880s this traffic had increased dramatically, and since the Crooked River had a deep entrance, with some eighteen feet of water at the bar, officials saw potential here for a large port. So the board made plans to replace the wrecked Dog Island Light with a mainland lighthouse to be built near the mouth of the river.

In 1889 the board sought and received $40,000 from Congress to construct a skeleton-style iron tower on the banks of the Crooked River, but the money was not put to use until nearly five years later. Confusion over title to the land and other delays kept workmen away from the construction site until late in 1894. Once underway, though, work progressed so swiftly that the lantern and fixtures were in place by October 1895.

The tower lifted the lantern's fourth-order lens 115 feet above sea level, high enough for the light to be seen from sixteen miles away. The revolving lens showed two flashes every ten seconds. The Crooked River Lighthouse, its lower half painted white and upper half painted dark red, remains in use today.

Hurricanes continue to pound this stretch of the Gulf Coast. Homes and summer cottages built on Dog Island are often placed on stilts to raise them above the inevitable flood tides that accompany major storms. Even so, man-made structures on this and other barrier islands are threatened by the shifting of the land itself. After every hurricane geologists—and some

A close-up view of the lantern and gallery at the top of the century-old Crooked River tower.

startled home owners as well—find that Dog Island has moved a little more to the west, placing some houses and property in the water.

Most barrier islands on the Gulf and other U.S. coasts came into existence only since the end of the last ice age, about 10,000 ago. As marginal lands they are ephemeral and likely to disappear into the sea as suddenly as they emerged from it. Anything built on the islands should be considered temporary—as the destruction of the Dog Island Lighthouse in 1873 dramatically illustrates.

The Crooked River Lighthouse was designed with the special geology and weather conditions of the Gulf Coast in mind. Unlike the original Dog Island tower, which was made of brick, its open skeleton structure allows hurricane-force winds to pass through, doing little damage. Built on more stable ground on the mainland, the 1895 tower has stood now for more than a century and continues to serve mariners.

HOW TO GET THERE:

The lighthouse can be seen from US–98, a few miles west of Carrabelle. A dirt road leads to the tower, located a few hundred yards off the highway. The tower is not open to the public, and there are no facilities of any kind. However, the tall red-and-white tower soaring toward the sky is an inspiring sight.

CAPE ST. GEORGE LIGHT

St. George Island, Florida – 1833 and 1852

Steamboats were once able to ply the fabled Apalachicola and Chattahoochee Rivers all the way to Columbus, Georgia, some 300 miles inland. Reaching far into the southern agricultural heartland, the steamers turned these wide, blue waterways into rivers of cotton and made the town of Apalachicola one of the busiest ports on the Gulf Coast. Freighters from Europe and the U.S. East Coast streamed into Apalachicola Bay and dropped anchor to await their turn at the cotton-loading docks. To guide these vessels into the bay, the government established a light station on St. George Island in 1833.

Famed lighthouse contractor Winslow Lewis built the seventy-foot brick tower for just under $9,500, fitting it with one of his own, patented lamp-and-reflector lighting systems. Located amid the shifting dunes of an unstable barrier island, the station was to have a relatively short life. Almost from the beginning, the facility was thought to be inadequate—a charge made against many of the lighthouses built by Lewis. It had a short range of only a few miles, and ships approaching from the east were unlikely to see it before slamming into the shallows off the southern end of the island—several cargo vessels were lost in just this way. Even so, more than fifteen years would pass before anything was done to improve the situation.

During the late 1840s, war with Mexico focused fresh attention on the needs of Gulf ports. Consequently, Congress finally provided funds for a new and better light tower on St. George Island. Using materials from the original tower, a local contractor built the new lighthouse for only $6,700 and had it ready for service late in 1848.

The new tower stood for less than three years. In August of 1851 a mighty gale descended on the Florida Panhandle, leveling the lighthouses at Cape San Blas and Dog Island as well as the recently completed brick tower of St. George Island. Rebuilt in 1852, the seventy-foot lighthouse tower on St. George Island had stood for only a few years when a storm came blasting out of the gulf and knocked it down. Rebuilt in 1852, the tower was fitted with a third-order lens that made the light visible more than fifteen miles at sea. This second tower proved much stronger or, perhaps, luckier than the first; it still stands

today, despite repeated assaults by hurricanes, gales, and Confederate guns.

During the Civil War the Confederates fired on the lighthouse and managed to put it out of service temporarily. But the damage was repaired and the light back in use again by the time the war ended in 1865. Not until 1889 did keepers notice a dark, angular crack in the lens, apparently put there by a well-aimed rebel shot.

Marking the western entrance to the Apalachicola Bay, the Cape St. George Lighthouse is in use today. Located on an isolated and uninhabited island, the automated light operates on battery power. The keeper's house and other outbuildings are in ruins, but the tower itself remains as tall and lovely as ever. The island is a fine place to hunt for sea-shells or, if you like, to be alone for a while.

During the late 1840s war with Mexico focused fresh attention on the needs of Gulf ports. Consequently, Congress finally provided funds for a new and better light tower on St. George Island. Using materials from the original tower, a local contractor built the new lighthouse for only $6,700 and had it ready for service late in 1848.

The new tower stood for less than three years. In August 1851 a mighty gale descended on the Florida Panhandle, leveling the lighthouses at Cape San Blas and Dog Island as well as the recently completed brick tower of St. George Island.

HOW TO GET THERE:

This isolated lighthouse, no longer an aid to navigation, stands on a remote island that can be reached only by boat. Since the island is not inhabited, visitors should take along drinking water and food. For information and advice on transportation, call the Division of Natural Resources in Apalachicola at (904) 653–9419. To protect the natural turtle habitat, special permission must be obtained to visit the area surrounding the lighthouse. For more information on access to this scenic area, contact the St. George Island State Park, P.O. Box 62, Eastpoint, FL 32328; (904) 670–2111.

The Cape St. George Lighthouse, as it looked before recent storms nearly toppled it. Only a narrow strip of sand now holds back the Gulf.

CAPE SAN BLAS LIGHT

Cape San Blas, Florida – 1847, 1856, and 1885

A few miles west of the Apalachicola River, the Florida panhandle juts out into the Gulf. Here, sand and silt churned up by swirling currents have formed an angular navigational obstacle called Cape San Blas. The same natural process that built the cape also created a series of dangerous shoals extending four to five miles out into the Gulf. Constantly shifting and frequently raked by powerful storms, the shoals are a sailor's nightmare. Keeping a light on the cape to warn away ships has likewise proved a nightmare for lighthouse officials.

The Cape San Blas Lighthouse had stood for only four years when, in 1851, it fell in a hurricane—the same giant storm that knocked down the tower at Cape St. George. It took fever-plagued construction crews five years to rebuild the San Blas tower, but its light had shown for only a few months when a gale pushed it over again.

Undeterred, the Lighthouse Board put crews to work once more and had the light back in operation just in time for the Civil War. Confederate raiders hit the cape almost as hard as a hurricane, burning down the keeper's house and torching everything combustible—even the doors and window sashes in the lighthouse tower.

Relighted after the war, the light was in trouble again by the late 1870s. This time the threat was erosion—the Gulf was eating away the cape. By 1880 the surf had reached the base of the lighthouse, and within two years the tower stood in eight feet of water. Its foundation undermined by seawater, the tower began to settle, leaning further toward the Gulf each day. Finally, it could no longer keep its balance and crashed down into the waves.

The board now made plans for yet another lighthouse at Cape San Blas, this one of a type far less susceptible to high winds and water. Instead of a brick-and-mortar tower, it would have a lightweight iron skeleton held together by struts and wires. While the skeleton was under construction at a shipyard in the North, a small light placed on the end of a long pole did the work of alerting ships' crews to the danger of the shoals. This makeshift arrangement continued for longer than anyone had expected, since the ship ferrying the prefabricated skeleton to the Gulf sank near Sanibel Island, south of Tampa Bay.

Somehow, the board managed to salvage its iron tower and by 1885 had it in place about 500 feet from the beach on Cape San Blas. But the Gulf continued its landward march, often chewing up the cape at the astounding rate of one foot each day. The light had to be moved twice more; eventually the Gulf forced the board to move the tower almost a quarter of a mile north.

HOW TO GET THERE:

The Air Force has taken over the land on which the lighthouse is located and has closed it to the public. For any information on when it might be reopened, contact the Apalachicola Bay Chamber of Commerce, 45 Market Street, Apalachicola, Florida 32320.

ST. JOSEPH BAY LIGHT

Port St. Joe, Florida – 1837 and 1903

About midway along the 150-mile length of the Florida Panhandle, the land drops sharply to the south. From the apex of this prominent elbow, a long, thin peninsula swings westward and then northward, forming a bay some five miles wide and more than a dozen miles long. The protected waters of St. Joseph's Bay offered such excellent anchorage for ships that early Florida settlers thought the area almost certain to prosper. Following the acquisition of Florida by the United States, the town of St. Joseph, on the mainland side the bay, grew into a thriving port. Florida's first constitutional convention was held here in 1838.

That same year a lighthouse was built on the far tip of the peninsula, its fifty-foot tower marking the entrance to the bay. Produced by a Winslow Lewis lamp-and-reflector system, its beacon attracted a steady stream of ships and commerce. Then, in 1841, a visiting freighter brought yellow fever to St. Joseph, decimating the population. Before the town could recover, a hurricane swept in from the Gulf, leaving little of St. Joseph's docks, stores, and houses but a pile of splinters bobbing in the surf. So complete was the devastation that in 1847 the lighthouse itself was abandoned, its iron lantern removed for use at the light station on nearby Cape San Blas.

From the ruins of the once thriving community of St. Joseph, the village of Port St. Joe emerged, but more than half a century passed before the government thought it merited a lighthouse. Finally, in 1902, a square wooden dwelling and tower was built on the mainland, directly across from St. Joseph Point. The lantern, situated atop the peaked roof of the main building, held a third-order Fresnel lens. Its light could be seen from about thirteen miles away, and just as the earlier St. Joseph beacon had done, this one helped guide vessels into the bay.

The new station's first keeper was Charles Lupton, who, along with his wife, Minnie, dutifully managed the facility for more than twenty-six years. During the prohibition era, a rum-running freighter ran aground not far from the lighthouse, spilling many cases of illicit whiskey onto the beach. Before keeper Lupton could alert authorities, residents of Port St. Joe hurried to salvage the liquid cargo. No doubt, the rattling bottles of hooch, spirited away in wagons and Model T Fords, were used for medicinal purposes.

In 1960 the Coast Guard closed the St. Joseph Bay station, replacing its light with an automated beacon displayed from atop a steel tower resembling a broadcast antenna. The old lighthouse was sold off for use as a barn. Several years ago it was purchased and refurbished as a private residence.

HOW TO GET THERE:

From Port St. Joe, drive northwestward for 10 miles to Beacon Hill. The existing steel tower rises just to the west of Beacon Road. The site of the original station is nearby.

(Photo by Bob and Sandra Shanklin)

PENSACOLA LIGHT

Pensacola, Florida – 1824 and 1858

Following the acquisition of Florida from Spain in 1819, the U.S. naval presence in the Gulf of Mexico increased dramatically. American warships cruised the dark, sparsely settled coast, discouraging smugglers and flushing out nests of pirates. But with their nearest base on the Eastern Seaboard, literally thousands of sea miles away, these fighting ships and their crews might as well have been operating in foreign waters. In 1824 the U.S. Navy moved to remedy this situation by establishing its first Gulf Coast deep-water base at Pensacola. That same year a lighthouse was erected to guide warships in and out of Pensacola's excellent harbor, which, with thirty-six feet of water, was one of the deepest on the Gulf.

The lighthouse tower was only forty feet tall, but it stood on a forty-foot bluff, giving it an effective height of eighty feet. Even so, sea captains frequently complained that the beam was obscured by tall trees. And the light itself was weak; in 1851 congressional investigators found

it "deficient in power, being fitted only with ten lamps and sixteen-inch reflectors." These inadequacies made it little more useful than a small harbor light.

The commandant of the Pensacola Naval Station repeatedly urged Congress to provide the harbor with a "first-class seacoast light." Finally, in 1858, he got his wish. A massive brick tower, built at a cost of nearly $25,000, raised the lantern 210 feet above the sea so that its beacon could be seen up to twenty-one miles at sea.

Only a few years after its construction, the big tower became a target for Union gunners firing on Confederate artillerymen dug in around the lighthouse. Unable to keep the lighthouse out of Union hands, the men in gray resorted to the tactic of stealing the lens and apparatus. These were hidden and not found until after the war.

The tower has also withstood bombardment by nature. It has been struck countless times by lightning; in 1875 a pair of bolts seared the lantern, melting and fusing metal parts in the apparatus. Ten years later an earthquake shook the structure so hard that the keeper imagined "people were ascending the steps, making as much noise as possible."

Despite the poundings it has taken, the Pensacola Lighthouse still stands. With its bottom third painted white and its top two-thirds painted black, the tower looks much as it has for more than one-hundred years. Its light, now automated, continues to lead navy ships and Coast Guard cutters into Pensacola Harbor.

HOW TO GET THERE:

The lighthouse, located at Pensacola Naval Air Station, can be reached by taking Navy Boulevard (State 295) south out of Pensacola. The station is an open post, and the guard at the gate can provide a car pass and directions to the lighthouse. Although the tower and the keeper's quarters are not open to the public, visitors can tour the grounds, which are open daily (except holidays) from 9:00 A.M. to 5:00 P.M. The lighthouse complex has several other buildings, which are used to store lamp oil and supplies. The complex is in remarkably good condition, probably because it has been protected on the base and maintained by the Coast Guard.

CHAPTER THREE

Lights of
THE SPANISH SHOALS
ALABAMA *and* MISSISSIPPI

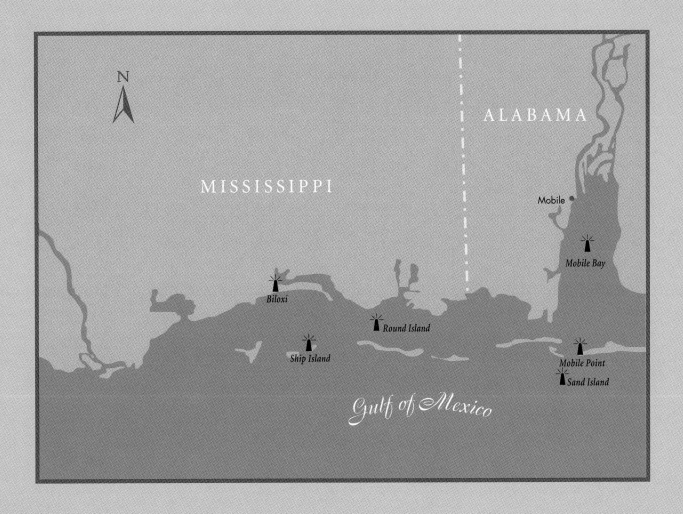

N

ALABAMA

MISSISSIPPI

Mobile

Mobile Bay

Biloxi

Round Island

Ship Island

Mobile Point

Sand Island

Gulf of Mexico

Anchored by screw piles to the bottom of Mobile Bay, iron legs provide support for the six-sided cottage of Mobile Bay Light. Local donations and a federal grant helped save the historic structure after the Coast Guard abandoned it in the 1960s.

*L*a Balize, the first lighthouse ever built on the Gulf Coast, had stood for only a dozen years when a 1778 hurricane swept over the Louisiana marshes. After the storm nothing was left of the light tower or of the small town that had stood nearby. No one knows what happened to the keepers or the residents of La Balize village, but it is easy to imagine. The same sort of tragedy would strike the Gulf Coast many times in the centuries that followed. Hurricane Alley can be a very dangerous place—for lighthouses and people.

The hurricane that struck St. Marks in 1843 left the keeper and his family in no doubt that their lives were at an end. Waves slammed against the walls of the dwelling, and the mounting tides drove them into the tower, where they climbed the steps to escape the rising waters. Somehow they survived. Far less lucky were more than a dozen other island residents who, when the storm finally passed, had simply vanished. The same storm converted the nearby town of St. Joseph to driftwood.

The storm also devastated the light station at Apalachicola but did little damage to the Dog Island Lighthouse. There was nothing left on Dog Island for the storm to ruin—all traces of its lighthouse had been obliterated in a hurricane the year before. Eventually, the Dog Island beacon would shine again, but the new forty-foot wooden tower met the same fate as its predecessor—a gale bowled it over in 1851. As if heeding the lesson of the "Three Little Pigs" nursery story, the Lighthouse Board used brick when they rebuilt it a second time, but they might just as well have used straw. When a monster storm descended on the Gulf Coast in September 1873, the keeper and his assistant managed to get off Dog Island just ahead of the tidal surge. When they returned, nothing remained of their station. Even the iron lantern had been washed out to sea. The Dog Island Lighthouse was never rebuilt.

Brick from the storm-blasted St. Joseph's Point Lighthouse was used to build the nearby Cape San Blas light station. Completed in 1848, its tower stood for just three years before being blown over in the 1851 hurricane that smashed the Dog Island station—the mid-1800s were not a good time to live on the Gulf Coast. The replacement tower lasted less than five years. A fourteen-foot floodtide accompanying an 1856 summer gale bulldozed the site. Following the storm the keeper, who had somehow survived the disaster, reported that he could see only a lagoon where his lighthouse had once stood.

Cape San Blas seemed unable to decide whether it was part of the ocean or dry land. After the station was rebuilt on slightly higher ground—the construction crews were constantly harassed by storms—waves steadily cut away at the beach until they reached the foundation of the tower. Completely undermined, it finally collapsed in 1882. The ship carrying materials to build a replacement tower for this hard-luck lighthouse sank off the south Florida coast. Most of the essential parts were recovered by salvagers, and the new station was completed by 1885, but that was not the end of its saga. Every few years a major Gulf storm would remove or replace sections of the cape, playing "now you see it, now you don't" with the lighthouse grounds. Hurricanes in 1915 and 1916 made an island of the station, placing it more than 200 yards offshore. Luckily, the iron skeleton of the 1885 tower was designed so that it could be taken apart easily and reassembled at a new location—much as the Gulf does with the cape itself—whenever necessary.

Low-lying coastal lands along the Gulf Coast are notoriously fickle and prone to vanish or reappear after major gales. One of the most astounding—and tragic—disappearances took place in 1906, when a killer hurricane swept over the Sand Island Light Station off Mobile Point, Alabama. On the day before the storm, the lighthouse had stood on an island. On the day after, the island was gone and along with it the dwelling, keeper Andrew Hansen, and his wife. Only the 132-foot brick tower remained, and it was now separated from the nearest dry land by more than a quarter of a mile of choppy water.

The dark shell of the long-abandoned Sand Island Lighthouse rises out of the waters near the entrance to Mobile Bay. A killer 1906 hurricane washed away the island itself.

The tropical behemoth that washed away Sand Island in 1906 was one of the most powerful and deadly hurricanes in history. At Round Island Light Station it sent waves crashing to the top of the fifty-foot tower. Driven up the tower steps to escape the rising waters, keeper Thorwald Hansen finally saved himself by taking refuge in his final redoubt—the lantern room. The keeper of the Horn Island Lighthouse was not so fortunate, however. When a rescue party finally made it to the island after the storm, they found no trace of the station, keeper Charles Johnson, or his family. Six feet of water now covered much of the island, including the site of the former lighthouse.

Even lighthouses far from the open waters of the Gulf are not immune from gales. The Lake Borgne Lighthouse in Louisiana lost its roof to a hurricane in 1893. Although it was well away from the main track of the storm, the 1906 hurricane blew its roof off once again and so damaged the station that it had to be completely rebuilt. A hurricane wrecked the Bayou St. John Lighthouse in 1860. A year or so later, occupying Union troops would complete the destruction. By the end of the war, only its pilings remained.

Just as the keeper of the Bolivar Point Lighthouse at Galveston had three years earlier, the keeper of the Port Pontchartrain Lighthouse near New Orleans served heroically during and after the 1903 Louisiana hurricane. Mrs. Margaret Norvell, the widow of a former keeper, became a guardian angel for more than 200 storm refugees who gathered at the light station for protection from the wind, high water, and poisonous snakes driven out of the bayous by the tides. The storm flattened every building in Port Pontchartrain except the light tower. A dozen years later a second mighty hurricane struck the area, this one sending barometers plunging to an all-time low for mainland America—28.11 inches of mercury. Mrs. Norvell again played the hero by aiding storm victims, as did Caroline Riddle, keeper of the nearby New Canal Lighthouse. The lights at both stations were kept burning throughout the storm.

An old-fashioned weathervane atop the Biloxi Lighthouse indicates the wind direction. On several occasions hurricane-force winds have battered this historic tower and the lovely coastal community it serves.

MOBILE BAY LIGHT

Mobile Bay, Alabama – 1885

uilt in a style used frequently in the Chesapeake Bay, the Mobile Bay Lighthouse consists of a hexagon-shaped cottage with a lantern perched atop its roof. The structure rests on iron pilings screwed into the muddy floor of the bay.

Although quite similar in style, the Mobile Bay Lighthouse proved much more difficult to build than its cousins in the Chesapeake. The iron skeleton that was to hold the lighthouse above the shallow waters of the bay was prefabricated in the North and shipped by sea to Alabama without incident. The trouble began when crews had to erect the skeleton on its pilings far out in the bay. Located in the very middle of the bay, the construction site was exposed to the worst weather the Gulf could throw at it. Gales hindered crews, and on more than one occasion workmen had to flee for their lives to the Alabama mainland.

While still under construction, the lighthouse began to sink into the sticky mud at the bottom of the bay. Before long it had lost more than seven feet of its height; but since the settling was evenly distributed, the structure remained sound. The board ordered the light placed in service, and it first shined on December 1, 1885, displaying a white light with red flashes every thirty seconds.

Although five additional lighthouses were planned to mark the serpentine channels through the bay, no more were built. The original cottage lighthouse has stood now for more than a century, a lone sentinel at the heart of Mobile Bay. Although its lamp has been extinguished for many years, ships continue to use the Mobile Bay Lighthouse as a daymark. The Coast Guard intended to demolish the structure in 1967, but spirited public opposition prevented its removal.

Two other lighthouses once marked the channels leading into the bustling port of Mobile. The first rose from Choctaw Point on the western side of the bay, the second from Battery Gladden, an artificial island originally used as a Confederate gun emplacement. Built in 1830 on a muddy bank only inches above high water, the brick Choctaw Point tower placed its light forty-three feet above the bay. The structure had been poorly sited, however, and was of little use to mariners. The lighthouse was located so far from the deep-water channel that ships moving up and down the bay could barely see either the tower or its beacon. Sailors who frequented Mobile Bay were not displeased when a hurricane blasted the station in 1858, forcing the government to abandon it.

The far more violent man-made storm of war descended on Mobile and the entire nation before the Choctaw Point light station could be replaced. In fact, the project was not undertaken until several years after the

Confederate guns at Fort Morgan (above) failed to stop Farragut's Union gunboats. The Battery Gladden Lighthouse (below) once stood on the site of a key Confederate artillery position. (Photo below courtesy U.S. Coast Guard)

end of the Civil War. Instead of rebuilding the practically useless mainland tower, lighthouse officials opted for a midchannel structure of a screwpile design similar to that later employed for the Middle Bay Lighthouse. Completed in 1872, the hexagonal dwelling and tower stood in open water beside Battery Gladden. The new station had a fourth-order Fresnel lens displaying a white light with a red sector to guide ships around a key turning point in the channel. The Battery Gladden Lighthouse served until 1913, by which time improvements in the channel had rendered it unnecessary. Afterwards the building slowly rotted away, finally collapsing into the bay in 1951.

HOW TO GET THERE:

Located in the middle of Mobile Bay, the spiderlike lighthouse is a popular destination for day boaters. Handsomely restored and maintained by the Alabama Historical Commission, the cottage-style lighthouse still serves as a daymark for vessels moving in and out of Mobile Harbor. For more information contact the Mobile Visitors Bureau, One South Water Street, P.O. Box 204, Mobile, AL 36601; (334) 415–2000 or (800) 5MO–BILE. For additional information on travel in coastal Alabama, contact the Alabama Visitors Bureau at (800) 745–7263.

MOBILE POINT LIGHT

Mobile, Alabama – 1822, 1873, and 1966

Although Mobile Bay is a substantial body of water more than twenty miles long and ten miles across, its entrance is restricted. Ships moving into the bay from the open waters of the Gulf of Mexico are forced into narrow channels by a wall of barrier islands and a maze of shoals, shallows, and sandbars. The primary channel passes a spit of sand known as Mobile Point.

The strategic natures of the spit and the broad bay behind it were not lost on the U.S. government when it took control of the area from the Spanish in 1821. The ink

(Photo by Bob and Sandra Shanklin)

on the treaty with Spain granting possession of Florida and much of the Gulf Coast was barely dry when U.S. troops started building Fort Morgan at Mobile Point to protect this new American possession. On the grounds of the fort a lighthouse was raised to guide ships through the tricky passages into the bay and spur commercial development.

Completed in 1822, the station's forty-foot brick tower and lamp-and-reflector lighting system cost $9,995, a steep price for a lighthouse at that time. In sharp contrast to the cost of the structure itself, the Fort Morgan soldier assigned to tend the light was paid only $15 a month. Not surprisingly, maintenance of the light was shoddy. What was worse, despite the money poured into its planning and construction, the finished light could be seen from only ten miles away and gave scant warning of shoals that lay up to nine miles from shore.

To solve the maintenance problem, officials appointed a civilian keeper to tend the light. Well-known lighthouse contractor Winslow Lewis was brought in to find a way to strengthen the beacon. Lewis installed new, more powerful lamps and larger reflectors, placing them on a rotating bed to make the light flash. This flashing light was, in fact, much brighter and easier to see, but maritime authorities inexplicably neglected to inform mariners of the change. More than one confused sea captain nearly wrecked his vessel before realizing that the Mobile Point Light no longer displayed a fixed beacon.

When Alabama seceded from the Union at the beginning of the Civil War, the state laid claim to all federal property on its soil, including, of course, mighty Fort Morgan and its lighthouse. As with lighthouses elsewhere along Confederate coasts, the station's lens was dismantled and removed for safe storage until the end of the war.

With its powerful cannon, the fort remained an obstacle to federal naval forces for much of the war. Not until August 1864 did Union warships finally manage to run past the fort and into the bay. It was then, during the decisive Battle of Mobile Bay, that Union Admiral David Farragut issued his famous order: "Damn the torpedoes, full speed ahead!" The admiral might just as well have said

"Damn the lighthouse!" Artillery fire from federal gunboats and forces besieging Fort Morgan soon blasted the brick structure to rubble. A month would pass, however, before they managed to capture the stubbornly defended fortress itself.

With the fort and lighthouse in ruins, a temporary light served Mobile Point until 1873, when a thirty-five-foot steel tower was built atop the broken walls. Fitted with a fourth-order Fresnel lens, it displayed a red light with a focal plane approximately fifty feet above high water. In 1966 this light was discontinued and replaced by a 125-foot, antennalike tower built hard by the walls of the historic fort. Despite the untraditional—some might say ugly—looks of the present tower, its flashing white light efficiently guides ships in and out of Mobile Bay.

After the old, 1873 tower was decommissioned in 1966, its metal skeleton was sold to a salvage company as scrap—an all-too-typical display of bureaucratic insensitivity to history. Fortunately, local preservationists protested, and the little tower was returned to the fort where it stands today, a monument to two centuries of tradition.

HOW TO GET THERE:

From Mobile follow Interstate 10 east to exit 44. Then follow Route 59 South to Gulf Shores and turn westward on Route 180. Signs lead the way to the Fort Morgan State Historic Site, which is filled with fascinating Civil War and military displays. The 1873 tower and present antenna-style tower are located near one another beside the walls of the fort and offer a study in contrasting technologies. While in the area be sure to enjoy Alabama's extraordinary white beaches, but take care to turn off the road only in marked parking areas. Otherwise, your vehicle may end up stuck in the soft sand. For travel information call the Alabama Gulf Coast Visitors Bureau at (800) 745–7263.

SAND ISLAND LIGHT

Mobile Bay, Alabama – 1838, 1859, and 1872

The island for which this lighthouse was named no longer exists and, for that matter, neither does the light itself. The island long ago eroded and washed away, but the light was extinguished only recently—by a flood of modern shipboard navigational aids that made it unnecessary. Abandoned, isolated, and completely surrounded by the inky waters of Mobile Bay, the black Sand Island tower stands today only as a monument to its own violent and tragic past.

A fifty-five-foot tower was raised on the island in 1838 as a complement to the Mobile Point Light on the opposite side of the entrance to Mobile Bay. Relatively small for

a coastal lighthouse, it eventually proved unequal to its task, and plans were made to erect a much larger structure in its place. When completed in 1859, at a cost of $35,000, the new, 150-foot tower was crowned with a first-order lens that probably made the light visible from more than twenty miles at sea.

The big lighthouse would stand for little more than three years. It was destined to fall in the conflict that leveled so many other tall Americans, Northern and Southern, a victim of the Civil War. During the early months of the war, it was unclear who owned the huge lighthouse, which had been federal property, or who would benefit most from its guidance. Confederate officials had the enormous first-order lens dismantled and moved to shore for safekeeping.

Soon Union gunboats appeared off Mobile Bay, and Northern troops seized the Sand Island Light Station. A fourth-order lens was placed in the tower and the beacon reestablished late in December 1862. This weaker, but still useful, light would not shine for long, however. One month later a Confederate raiding party under Lieutenant John Glenn crossed over from the Southern stronghold at Fort Gaines and set fire to several station buildings. Artillery rounds from the Union gunboat USS *Pembroke* drove off the raiders before they could damage the tower itself. Undeterred, Glenn swore he would return and "tumble the lighthouse down in their teeth." Not given to idle boasts, Glenn kept his dark promise little more than three weeks later.

On February 23, 1862, Glenn and his raiders struck the light station again. This time they placed a seventy-pound gunpowder bomb at the base of the tower, lit the fuse, and ran for cover. The explosion came quickly, and falling bricks and masonry from the collapsing tower nearly killed the young lieutenant. Ironically, Glenn would later proudly deliver his official report on the tower's destruc-tion to Confederate General Danville Leadbetter. Just three years earlier Leadbetter had been the federal engineer who designed and built the Sand Island tower.

After the war the station's magnificent first-order lens was found safe and secure in Montgomery, Alabama. It was restored to its rightful place some years later when the Sand Island Lighthouse was rebuilt.

After the lighthouse was rebuilt during 1871–72 by a yellow fever–tormented work crew, the island beneath the structure began to erode. By 1896 the island beneath Alabama's first and only coastal lighthouse had completely disappeared. During the next ten years, the island reappeared several times, only to vanish in the next storm. Then, in 1906, a hurricane washed it away forever.

Unfortunately, the storm carried away more than just the sand. After the hurricane had passed inland and the winds had died down, a worried lighthouse inspector hurried out to check on the Sand Island Light Station and its keepers. Later, the inspector sent this telegram to his superiors: "Sand Island Light out. Island washed away. Dwelling gone. Keepers not to be found."

HOW TO GET THERE:

Although its light has been extinguished and the island it stands on is inundated, this storm-battered tower still stands. Surrounded by water, it can be reached only by boat. Dauphin Island, the closest place to launch a boat, can be reached by driving south from Mobile on State 163. For more information call the Alabama Gulf Coast Visitors Bureau at (800) 745–7263 or contact the Mobile Visitors Bureau, One South Water Street, P.O. Box 204, 36601; (334) 415–2000 or (800) 5MO–BILE.

ROUND ISLAND LIGHT

Pascagoula, Mississippi – 1833 and 1859

French explorers gave Round Island its name (Isle Ronde) because of its circular shape. Actually, modern charts show it to be shaped like a teardrop. Over the years more than a few shipowners have shed tears over the loss of their vessels on nearby shoals. To warn mariners of this danger and guide ships through the Mississippi Sound and to the bustling port of Pascagoula, the Lighthouse Service established a light station on Round Island in 1833.

The entire station, including the tower, keeper's dwelling, lamps, and reflectors, cost the government less than $6,000. Built on ground only about three feet above sea level, the forty-five-foot brick tower was vulnerable to both flooding and erosion. Even so, it survived a number of hurricanes and powerful gales.

The station was almost destroyed, however, during an invasion of Round Island in 1849 by a small army of adventurers. Bent on freeing Cuba from the Spanish, several hundred lightly armed soldiers of fortune set up camp on the island to prepare for their expedition. While the keeper was away purchasing supplies on the mainland, they vandalized the tower and dwelling. U.S. troops sent to evict the freebooters mistakenly arrested the hapless keeper when he returned to the island with his beans, pork, and other provisions. Luckily, the keeper had on hand a copy of his official appointment. His identity confirmed, the keeper was released and the freebooters dispersed, but not before the station had sustained considerable damage.

By the mid-1850s the recently formed Lighthouse Board concluded that the station's tower had been built in the wrong place. Undercut by tidal erosion and exposed to constant pounding by storms blowing out of the east, it was sure to topple over in the next big hurricane. So, a new, fifty-foot tower was built on a higher and drier part of the island to the northwest of the original structure. Fitted with a fourth-order Fresnel lens, it served well until the Civil War darkened lights along the entire Gulf Coast. Following the war, the Round Island Light Station returned to active duty.

Over the years the tower has stood up to numerous major storms and hurricanes. Perhaps the worst crisis came in 1906, when a hurricane threw twenty-foot breakers against the tower walls. Huddled inside the tower, Keeper Thorwald Hansen survived the storm. Five keepers at light stations elsewhere along the Gulf Coast did not.

The Coast Guard automated the light in 1944 and then discontinued it two years later. The city of Pascagoula now owns the lighthouse, and a complete restoration is underway. The Round Island Lighthouse is listed on the National Register of Historic Places.

HOW TO GET THERE:

Round Island and its historic lighthouse can be reached only by boat. For information on charters and accessibility, contact the Pascagoula Chamber of Commerce, P.O Box 480, Pascagoula, MS 39568–0480; (228) 762–3391.

(Photo by Bob and Sandra Shanklin)

SHIP ISLAND LIGHT

Ship Island, Mississippi – 1853, 1886, and 1971

Before he became president of the Confederacy, Jefferson Davis enjoyed a long career in the U.S. Congress. Like other Congressmen, Davis worked overtime trying to secure federal facilities to boost the economy of his home state—Mississippi. As early as 1846 Davis was hounding his fellow representatives and senators to vote for his pet project, a fort and naval base on Ship Island, about a dozen miles off the Mississippi coast.

To quiet Davis the Congress appropriated $12,000 to build a lighthouse there instead. Completed in 1853, this handsome facility had a forty-five-foot brick tower and spacious keeper's dwelling. Although the lantern initially was fitted with an outmoded lamp-and-reflector lighting system, it received a state-of-the-art fourth-order Fresnel lens just three years later.

Eventually, Ship Island would get a substantial military installation as well, but it was definitely not the one Davis had wanted. By 1861 Davis had become the Confederate president, and late that year he was dismayed to learn that Union troops backed by a powerful fleet of warships had seized the island. In the face of this overwhelming assault, the handful of Confederate defenders destroyed the light station and burned the tower before decamping for the mainland. Union forces desperately needed the light to assist their naval blockade of Mississippi ports, and they quickly repaired the damage. The Southerners had dismantled and carted off the station's Fresnel lens as they left, but the Union sailors found a replacement lens in a captured warehouse on Lake Ponchartrain. The Ship Island Light burned for the remainder of the war, but its beacon showed only on its southern side, facing the open waters of the Gulf. The Union keepers blacked the north-facing windows so the light would be of no use to Confederate raiders and blockade runners.

The Ship Island Lighthouse saw such hard service during the war and the years immediately after that it literally began to fall apart. Inspectors declared the building unsafe, and in 1886 it was intentionally pulled down and a new wooden tower built to replace it. A pyramidal frame structure, it was covered by protective weatherboarding. Surprisingly long-lived for a wooden building on the humid Gulf of Mexico, it survived until 1972, when it burned to the ground in a fire accidentally set by tourists. A steel-skeleton tower took its place, and its light still guides mariners.

HOW TO GET THERE:

Ship Island, its light station, and historic Fort Massachusetts are all part of the Gulf Islands National Seashore. Still in remarkably good condition today, the fort was built by Union forces blockading the Mississippi coastline. Although the beacon remains active, not much remains of the old Ship Island Light Station. But visitors here will be doubly rewarded by some of America's finest ocean scenery. The seashore offers more than 50 miles of sparkling white beaches as well as facilities for primitive camping, fishing, and swimming. The seashore's visitors' center is located on the mainland at Ocean Springs. For more information on the seashore and advice on transportation to the islands, contact Gulf Islands National Seashore, 3500 Park Road, Ocean Springs, MS 39564; (904) 934–2604.

(Photo from the collection of Lamar C. Bevil, Jr.)

BILOXI LIGHT

Biloxi, Mississippi – 1848

Often located on empty barrier islands or remote spits of sand, lighthouses are frequently isolated and hard to reach. Not so the Biloxi Light. Its white, forty-eight-foot tower sits sandwiched between the eastbound and westbound lanes of U.S. Highway 90.

The brick-and-mortar tower is sheathed in a cast-iron shell. This design has proved a successful one and has enabled the tower to survive countless Gulf storms, including the infamous Hurricane Camille in 1968.

In the late 1860s the tower was painted black, and legend has it that this was done as a sign of mourning for President Lincoln. It is an unlikely story, especially when one considers that from the tower you can see Beauvoir, the home of Jefferson Davis, who, as president of the Confederacy, was Lincoln's most implacable enemy.

After the Civil War beach erosion threatened the lighthouse, causing it to lean a full two feet off the perpendicular. In a desperate attempt to save the structure, workers excavated soil from beneath the tower on the side away from the lean. Almost miraculously, their fight to save the tower succeeded, and it settled back into plumb.

For more than half a century, the Biloxi Lighthouse was kept by a woman. Maria Youghans became keeper in 1867 and only retired in 1920—when her daughter took over the job.

HOW TO GET THERE:

This lighthouse stands in the median strip of U.S.–90 at the foot of Porter Avenue in Biloxi. It is the only lighthouse in the South located on a major highway, and it's right in the middle of it—a marker for motorists as well as seamen.

The tower is now owned and maintained by the city of Biloxi. The lighthouse is open to the public when the weather permits. It is also open at other times by appointment. Weekend tours may be arranged by calling the Biloxi Recreation Department at (601) 435–6293.

The Biloxi Light stands within sight of Beauvoir, home of Jefferson Davis, president of the Confederacy.

CHAPTER FOUR

Lights of
THE WESTERN RIM

LOUISIANA and TEXAS

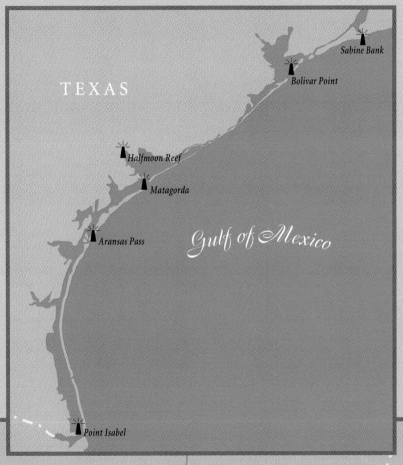

TEXAS

Sabine Bank

Bolivar Point

Halfmoon Reef

Matagorda

Aransas Pass

Gulf of Mexico

Point Isabel

TEXAS

LOUISIANA

Pass Manchac

Tchefuncte River

West Rigolets

New Canal

Port Pontchartrain
New Orleans

Chandeleur Island

Sabine Pass

Southwest Reef

Pass a l'Outre

Franks Island

South Pass

N

Gulf of Mexico

Ship Shoal

Timbalier Bay

Southwest Pass

The New Canal Light on Lake Pontchartrain still burns. Its dwelling is now a Coast Guard station.

The Mississippi River is one of the world's mightiest waterways. Drawing from the Missouri, the Ohio, the Arkansas, the Red, and countless small tributaries, it drains more than a third of the United States, pouring an average of 640,000 square feet of water into the Gulf of Mexico every second. That amounts to a cubic mile of water about every two and one-half days. Along with all this water comes vast quantities of eroded soil and rock, some of it brought from thousands of miles upstream and most of it dumped into Louisiana's spongy marshlands. It may not be too much to say that much of the state started out as part of the Rocky Mountains or the Appalachians.

Near where it ends its 2,500-mile journey in the southeastern reaches of Louisiana, the river has created a swampy netherworld, a region belonging neither to sea nor dry land. There, through an ever-changing maze of winding bayous and muddy passes, it finally reaches the Gulf. It almost seems the river is trying to keep its marriage to the Gulf of Mexico a secret. Perhaps this is why the mouth of the Mississippi was first discovered, not by a mariner sailing from the south out of the Gulf but by an explorer coming from the north out of the very heart of the continent.

DOWN THE MISSISSIPPI TO THE GULF OF MEXICO

It was the French nobleman Sieur de La Salle who first reached the river's mouth in 1682, after an extraordinary year-long trek through the Great Lakes and then down the great river itself by raft. Astonished when the wide, muddy river dumped him at long last into the Gulf of Mexico, La Salle marked the river mouth with a wooden sign bearing his own coat of arms. Doubtless, the sign was of little use to mariners hoping to find the river, but in time the French masters of Louisiana replaced it with more substantial daymarks, perhaps even a tower with a light to guide navigators at night. The small community that grew up around this tower was called "La Balize," or *seamark*.

More than eighty years after La Salle first visited the place, La Balize would become the site of the first true lighthouse on the Gulf of Mexico. By that time Louisiana was under the rule of Spain, and in 1767 Governor Antonio Ullola ordered a pyramidal tower built at the mouth of the Mississippi for use as a "pharos" or lighthouse. It was a handsome structure, and according to the governor's own reckoning, its light could be seen from up to ten miles at sea. Little more than ten years later, Ullola's pyramid suffered the same fate of many later Gulf Coast light-

Only an ugly stump remains of the Winslow Lewis tower on Franks Island, once the most important lighthouse on the Gulf. (Photo by Bob and Sandra Shanklin)

houses—it was utterly destroyed by a hurricane. In time the Spanish built a replacement tower, only to see it sink steadily and irretrievably into the mud. The Mississippi Delta is not friendly to man-made structures, a lesson that more than a few lighthouse designers and keepers would eventually learn the hard way.

In 1803 the U.S. government, under the leadership of President Thomas Jefferson, bought the entire 827,192-square-mile Louisiana Territory—today's state of Louisiana is, of course, much smaller. By that time this vast expanse of plains, rivers, lakes, and mountains was back in the hands of the French, who as usual were at war with the British and strapped for cash. The selling price the French accepted—$15 million, or less than three cents per acre—made the Louisiana Purchase one of history's all-time great bargains. Annual revenues from the territory would soon exceed the entire purchase price.

THE INCREDIBLE SINKING LIGHTHOUSES

The first lighthouse built in Louisiana by the United States would not prove such a bargain. As early as 1804, just after the territory became American soil, a lighthouse was envisioned for Frank's Island, at that time near the Mississippi's primary entrance. The plans drawn up for the structure by noted architect Benjamin Latrobe—he had designed the Capitol Building in Washington—proved so grandiose and impractical, however, that no contractor dared submit a bid for the project. An ornate Gothic Revival edifice, it included a palatial customs office and a tall light tower fashioned of brick, timber, and stone. There was even to be an ornate marble staircase. The entire complex would weigh many thousands of tons and almost certainly be swallowed up in the deep Mississippi mud. With no one willing to build Latrobe's architectural monstrosity

on the mosquito- and alligator-infested island, the project dragged on for years.

Then, into the picture stepped that hero of so many lighthouse-construction adventures—Winslow Lewis. The former New England sea captain told government bureaucrats that the structure Latrobe had designed was sure to fail, and quickly, but that he would happily build it for them for the breathtaking sum of $79,000. This was far more than had ever been spent on a lighthouse. To put the figure in perspective, consider that it was more than enough to buy three million acres of land at Louisiana Purchase prices. Such was the reputation of Latrobe and the befuddlement of U.S. officials, that in 1818 Lewis's outrageous bid was approved. Later that year Lewis and a

Now slowly sinking into the mud, the Pass a l'Outre Lighthouse once pointed the way to the Mississippi River. (Photo by Bob and Sandra Shanklin)

Each of the key Mississippi entrances, or passes, were marked by a lighthouse. Built in 1848, this Victorian tower dwelling guarded South Pass. (Courtesy U.S. Coast Guard)

crew of masons arrived at Frank's Island and dutifully executed the Latrobe design. Then they stood back and watched as the foundation declined, walls tilted, masonry cracked, and the whole thing fell to pieces. Lewis submitted his bill, and the horrified Treasury Department auditors then in charge of the Lighthouse Service had no choice but to smile and pay up.

At this point Lewis offered Treasury officials a deal they could not refuse. He would replace the lighthouse that now lay in a heap on Frank's Island with a far more practical structure for the bargain basement sum of $9,750. Lewis had the eighty-two-foot masonry tower built and in service by the spring of 1823. Its lamps and reflectors, designed by Lewis himself, produced a light that could be seen from nearly twenty miles away. Having groped blindly for the Mississippi entrance for so many years, mariners now had a light to follow. Lewis and his masons did their work so well that the Frank's Island tower still stands, but it is shorter than it used to be, having sunk more than twenty feet into the mud. In fact, the island itself sank. By the 1950s it had vanished altogether, leaving the old tower standing in ten feet of water.

The rust-covered skeletal remains of the Southwest Pass Lighthouse. Built in 1870, it cost the government $150,000, a truly enormous sum at the time. (Photo by Bob and Sandra Shanklin)

LIGHTS AT THE PASSES

Not only is the Mississippi secretive about the location of its primary outlet to the Gulf, it frequently changes its mind. Within a few years after the Frank's Island Light began guiding ships into the river's Northeast Pass, this waterway became too shallow for oceangoing vessels. Most navigators then opted for the deeper waters of the once secondary Pass a l'Outre (meaning "Pass Beyond" or "the Way Out"). The Frank's Island Lighthouse, which had cost the government so much consternation and expense, was discontinued and a new light station established at Pass a l'Outre. An iron tower, put in place by well-known lighthouse engineer Captain Danville Leadbetter, was fitted with a revolving Fresnel lens and was ready for service late in 1855.

Even as its flashing light began to guide ships into the river and onward to New Orleans or Baton Rogue, the Pass a l'Outre Lighthouse began a slow descent into the Mississippi Delta mud. Starting out about eighty-five feet tall, it would lose more than a quarter of its height—shrinking in stature to just sixty-two feet—before the station was discontinued in 1930. Long before that time, it had lost most of its usefulness to mariners. By the late 1880s Pass a l'Outre had filled with huge lumps of mud, making it almost impassable to ships.

Lighthouses were built on the banks of several other Mississippi River outlets, including South Pass and Southwest Pass, both completed by Winslow Lewis in 1832, and Head of Passes, first lit in 1836. All these waterways served at one time or another as primary entrances to the river—and all had a tendency to swallow up lighthouses.

The Coast Guard finally solved the sinking problem in 1965 with construction of the Southwest Pass Jetty Light. Built in open water atop large concrete supports, this modern light station resembles an off-shore oil rig, a likeness that has earned it the nickname "Texas Tower." Its aeromarine beacon has a focal plane more than eighty feet above the Gulf waters and can be seen from up to twenty-four miles away.

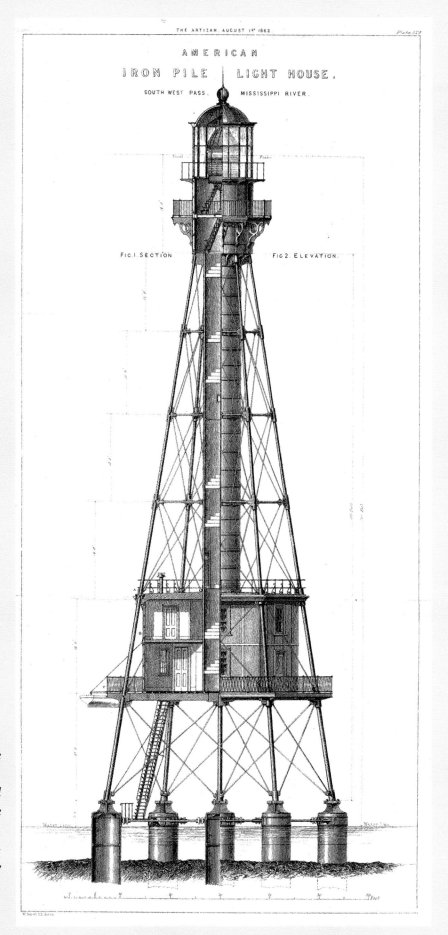

AMERICAN
IRON PILE LIGHT HOUSE.

SOUTH WEST PASS. MISSISSIPPI RIVER.

FIG.1 SECTION. FIG.2 ELEVATION.

An architect's drawing of the Southwest Pass tower raised on the Mississippi Delta mudflats in 1870. The cylindrical concrete-and-steel pilings were intended to keep the structure from sinking into the muck. The open steel supports allowed gale-force winds to pass harmlessly though the tower. (Diagram from private collection of Jim Claflin)

CHANDELEUR ISLAND LIGHT

Chandeleur Island, Louisiana – 1848, 1856, and 1896

In January 1815 General Andrew Jackson and his troops built defensive works with bales of cotton to prepare for an impending British assault on New Orleans. Meanwhile the British assembled an invasion fleet of more than fifty large transports and warships at Naso Roads, just inside Chandeleur Sound. When the attack finally came on January 8, the cotton walls and ramparts held, and the redcoats were driven back to their ships.

Over the years the vast anchorage in Chandeleur Sound has attracted far more commercial vessels than fighting ships. It lies on the direct route to New Orleans via Mississippi Sound. Despite their importance, however, neither the sound nor the long, fingerlike island chain that forms its outer wall were marked by a lighthouse until the mid-nineteenth century.

A lighthouse was finally established on the northern tip of Chandeleur Island in 1848. Its fifty-five-foot brick tower was surrounded by a seabreak of sand and shell to protect it from gales. But this wall provided far less defense against the sea than Andy Jackson's cotton wall had against the British. In 1852 hurricane tides swept over the wall and obliterated the station.

Yellow fever epidemics decimated the New Orleans labor force during the early 1850s, delaying reconstruction of the station for nearly three years. The new fifty-foot tower, crowned by a high-quality fourth-order Fresnel lens, was finally ready for service late in 1855. Seamen were happy to see the light shining once again. Not only did it mark a valuable anchorage and point the way to New Orleans, it also offered warning of the dangerous, spreading shoals in Chandeleur Sound.

Completed in 1895, the steel-skeleton tower seen here today was designed to better withstand high winds and water. Fitted with a third-order clamshell-type Fresnel lens, the tower stood 102 feet above mean sea level. The Coast Guard automated the light in 1966.

During the Prohibition era an invasion fleet gathered behind Chandeleur Island just as the British fleet had done more than a century before. These invaders were smugglers bent on delivering shiploads of liquor to thirsty New Orleans, where the concept of "dry" never had much meaning. Raids by Coast Guard cutters attempting to enforce prohibition laws often led panicky rumrunners to dump their cargoes, leaving the surface of Chandeleur Sound bobbing with bottles of illicit hooch.

(Photo by Bob and Sandra Shanklin)

HOW TO GET THERE:

Today, the still-active Chandeleur Lighthouse is part of the Breton National Wildlife Refuge. Established in 1904, it is the nation's second oldest federal wildlife refuge. Its 6,923 pristine acres feature an abundance of seabirds, including endangered brown pelicans. The lighthouse and refuge can be reached only by boat. For information on the refuge, call (504) 646–7555 or contact the U.S. Fish and Wildlife Service, Regional Director, 1875 Century Boulevard, Atlanta, GA 30345; (404) 679–4000.

PORT PONTCHARTRAIN LIGHT

New Orleans, Louisiana – 1832, 1839, and 1855

In 1832 a railroad and steamboat company financed a small, makeshift light tower to mark the artificial harbor recently built at Port Pontchartrain. The square lantern was hoisted up each night between two fifty-foot poles. The inadequacy of this arrangement lead to several wrecks near the port.

Under pressure from local politicians and business interests, the U.S. Congress appropriated funds to build a more conventional and effective lighthouse. Completed in 1839 at a cost of only $4,400, the new facility consisted of a twenty-eight-foot octagonal wooden tower with an iron lantern displaying a flashing white beacon.

The Lighthouse Board had the rotting wooden tower replaced by a conical concrete structure in 1855. Located nearly half a mile offshore, it rose more than forty feet above the lake. In 1857 the station's outmoded lamp-and-reflector lighting system was replaced by a compact fifth-order Fresnel lens.

Many of the keepers at this lighthouse were women. Keeper Margaret Norvell rode out the great hurricane of 1903 at the station while playing host to some 200 refugees driven from their homes by the rising waters. Mrs. W. E. Coteron was the station's keeper at the time it was discontinued in 1929.

Although inactive, the lighthouse still stands. Interestingly, the tower, once located far from dry land, is now located well inland. Land-hungry New Orleans developers have filled in large areas, extending the original shore far out into Lake Pontchartrain and leaving the little lighthouse high and dry.

HOW TO GET THERE:

The lighthouse is now on private land and is not open to the public. However, the nearby New Canal Lighthouse, now a Coast Guard rescue station, is accessible. It is located at the end of Lake Shore Boulevard near a series of marinas. Station personnel may have information on any changes in the status of the Port Pontchartrain tower. The docks near the Coast Guard station are lined with seafood restaurants. Do not leave the area without trying some fresh crab or red snapper. For information on these and endless other delights in the Big Easy, call the New Orleans—that's "Nawlins" to local folks—at (504) 566–5095.

(Photo by Lamar C. Bevil, Jr.)

NEW CANAL LIGHT

New Orleans, Louisiana – 1838, ca. 1855, and 1892

One of a series of inland lights that mark Louisiana's navigable lakes and bayous, the New Canal Lighthouse stands on the banks of Lake Pontchartrain, several miles north of downtown New Orleans. The lighthouse took its name from an ambitious, though failed, canal-building project begun during the early 1830s. Although the so-called New Canal was intended to link Pontchartrain with the New Orleans business district and with the Mississippi River, it was never completed. But while construction continued, a small, bustling harbor developed at the canal's terminus on Lake Pontchartrain.

In 1834 Congress provided $25,000, a considerable sum at that time, for a lighthouse to guide lake traffic in and out of the harbor. The lighthouse was probably made of brick, but despite that and its relatively high cost, it deteriorated rapidly. By 1854 the structure was considered unrepairable and had to be demolished.

It was soon replaced by a cottage-style lighthouse consisting of a lantern on the roof of a keeper's dwelling. Built for only $6,000, this new lighthouse survived the Civil War and remained in service for more than three decades.

The board discontinued the lighthouse in 1890 and sold the building at public auction. For more than a year the harbor was marked by a lantern hung from a high pole. Meanwhile, workmen erected the two-story, white-frame lighthouse that still stands beside the lake.

Today, only a few traces of the New Canal can be seen, but the lighthouse that bears its name remains active. The building that once doubled as a keeper's dwelling and lighthouse now serves as headquarters for the Coast Guard's Lake Pontchartrain rescue service. Answering more than 300 search-and-rescue calls per year, it is the busiest Coast Guard Station in the world.

HOW TO GET THERE:

Take I–10 and I–610 to the West End Boulevard North exit. Then take West End Boulevard to Lake Shore Boulevard and Lake Pontchartrain. The lighthouse is visible from Lake Shore Boulevard. Tours can be arranged with the Coast Guard by calling (504) 589–2331. Advanced notice is recommended.

TCHEFUNCTE RIVER LIGHT

Madisonville, Louisiana – 1838 and 1867

Just north of New Orleans, Lake Pontchartrain covers a vast expanse of inland Louisiana with a vast plain of water. Nowadays a toll causeway almost thirty miles long crosses the lake near its widest point, but during the nineteenth century, few could have imagined such a highway across the open water. Back then travel between the northern and southern shores of the lake was by boat.

The steamboats and freighters operating on the lake needed lights to guide them. Pontchartrain's north side, with its many dangerous shoals and mostly dark shoreline, was especially threatening. In 1837 the Lighthouse Service made navigation on Pontchartrain easier and safer by establishing a light station near Madisonville and the mouth of the Tchefuncte River.

It had been at Madisonville that a ragtag flotilla of gunboats assembled for action against the British fleet during the war of 1812. Shortly before the Battle of New Orleans in 1815, a British invasion force of some fifty warships trained their heavy guns on the little American fleet, converting it to splinters in a matter of minutes. Eventually, Madisonville would prosper, however, especially after the new lighthouse helped make it a bustling lake port.

Burned during the Civil War, the Tchefuncte River tower was rebuilt in 1867. The thirty-eight-foot tower still stands, and its light, automated during World War II, still guides lake traffic.

Since 1903 the Tchefuncte River beacon has served as a rear range light. Together with a secondary light placed below and some distance in front of the primary beacon, it marks a safe channel through the shallow lake. Navigators know the lights should appear one atop the other. When the top light tilts either to the left or right, the vessel is drifting out of the channel in the direction indicated.

HOW TO GET THERE:

From I–12 take exit 59 and follow Route 22 to Madisonville. Then follow signs to Fairview Riverside State Park and the lighthouse. An old fishing village, Madisonville is home to some of the best seafood restaurants in Louisiana. For more information contact the Madisonville Chamber of Commerce, P.O. Box 746, Madisonville, LA 70447; (504) 845–9824.

PASS MANCHAC LIGHT

Ponchatoula, Louisiana – 1837, 1842, 1846, 1859, and 1867

Built at about the same time as its neighbor, the Tchefuncte River Light Station near Madisonville, the Pass Manchac Light marked the western reaches of Lake Ponchartrain. The beacon guided vessels in and out of the narrow but vital Manchac Pass connecting the enormous lake with the smaller but still sizable Lake Maurepas.

Completed in 1839, the first Pass Manchac light tower lasted only three years. The masons who built it had used mud for mortar, which, not surprisingly, melted away in the heavy Louisiana rains. The tower literally fell to pieces. By 1842 it had been replaced by a better-quality structure, but the swirling waters of Lake Pontchartrain soon eroded the ground under the station, forcing construction of a third Pass Manchac Lighthouse. Built in 1846, its thirty-six-foot brick tower dutifully displayed a red light, but only for a few years. By about 1855 it, too, was in trouble. Its foundation began to sink into the mud, and the tower threatened to topple over into the lake. A fourth Pass Manchac tower was ready for service in early 1859, with little more than two years to spare before Civil War raiders brought ruin to the station once again.

The restored lighthouse returned to service in 1867, when it received an improved lantern, a fourth-order Fresnel lens, and a fine new brick keeper's dwelling. Luck was finally running with the station's rather than against it. Except for brief interruptions caused by storms, its light would shine every night for more than a century. Automated in 1952, it has since been deactivated.

HOW TO GET THERE:

Follow U.S. 51 north from La Place toward Ponchatoula. The tower stands on the north side of Pass Manchac. The dwelling and other station buildings were removed long ago.

Now abandoned, the Pass Manchac Lighthouse once marked a key channel linking Lake Pontchartrain with waters to the north and west. (Photo by Lamar C. Bevil, Jr.)

WEST RIGOLETS
LIGHTHOUSE

West Rigolets, Louisiana – 1855

Abandoned by the Coast Guard in 1945, the West Rigolets Lighthouse was left at the mercy of hurricanes and high water. Remarkably, the structure still stands. The station dates to 1855, when it was built on the shores of Lake Pontchartrain to guide vessels through a passage known as the Rigolets. Keeper Tom Harrison, shot to death in an 1862 attack by Confederate irregulars, was the only Lighthouse Service employee killed in the line of duty during the Civil War. Although in an advanced state of deterioration, the old building may soon be restored. The cisterns on the right once held the station's water supply.

TIMBALIER BAY LIGHT

Timbalier Bay, Louisiana – 1857 and 1875

Established during the 1850s to guide vessels through a stretch of shallow water once thought unnavigable, the Timbalier Bay Light Station was decommissioned and then relit several times. Obliterated by a hurricane after the Civil War, it was rebuilt in 1875. Its foundation pilings repeatedly sinking in the mud, the tower had to be rebuilt in 1881 and again in 1895. The present structure dates to 1917. Automated in 1934, the light was finally discontinued during the 1950s. It serves today as a daymark.

SOUTHWEST REEF LIGHT

Berwick, Louisiana – 1859

Completed in 1859, the iron-clad Southwest Lighthouse was built to withstand the fury of hurricanes blowing in from the Gulf. It was a storm of a very different type, however, that would put the station out of service little more than two years after it was established. With the outbreak of the Civil War, local Confederate officials ordered removal of the lens, lamps, and even the lantern's window glass. Union troops recaptured these items late in the war, and by August 1865 the station's light was once more shining.

Displaying a red light meant to warn vessels away from a dangerous reef in the Atchafalaya Bay, the 125-foot tower stood on screw piles in open water. Its exposed position placed it at the mercy of gales. An extraordinarily powerful hurricane struck the station in October 1867, throwing waves far up the side of the tower. Howling on for more than twenty-four hours, it broke through the floor of the dwelling, smashed the station landing platform and walkway, knocked down the gallery, and even bent the screw piles on which the tower stood. The crew survived only by hanging onto beams and girders.

Repaired after the storm for a cost of $10,000, the lighthouse served until 1916, when a dredging operation cut through the shoal. Afterwards the old tower stood rusting in the bay for nearly three-quarters of a century. Then, during the 1980s, the southern Louisiana town of Berwick brought the tower ashore for use as the primary attraction of a city park.

HOW TO GET THERE:

Berwick is located on U.S. 90 just west of Morgan City, Louisiana. The tower stands in Everett S. Berry Lighthouse Park, which can be reached via Bellevue Front Street and Canton Street. The lighthouse itself is not open to the public, but visitors are welcome to walk the grounds. The Berwick City Hall at 3225 Third Street, about two blocks from the Lighthouse Park, has on display a beautiful third-order Fresnel lens. For more information call (504) 384–8858.

The Southwest Reef Lighthouse is now proudly displayed by Berwick, Louisiana, in the town's unique Lighthouse Park. (Photo by Bob and Sandra Shanklin)

(Photo by Bob and Sandra Shanklin)

SHIP SHOAL LIGHT

Gulf of Mexico – 1859

The eight-legged Ship Shoal Lighthouse stands on screw piles in the open waters of the Gulf of Mexico, about fifteen miles from the Louisiana coast. It was built in 1858 to mark a threatening shoal on the heavily traveled trade route linking Texas ports with the Mississippi Delta region. The iron-skeleton tower was assembled in a Philadelphia foundry and shipped south to be erected on piles sunk deep into the shoal. Permanently discontinued in 1965, the abandoned tower still stands and is used by navigators as a daymark. The town of Berwick, Louisiana, hopes to bring the tower ashore eventually for use as the centerpiece of a park.

SABINE PASS LIGHT

Louisiana Point, Louisiana – 1856

Although the Sabine Pass Lighthouse was built several years before the Civil War, its finlike concrete buttresses give it a surprisingly modern appearance. Completed in 1856, the eighty-foot octagonal brick tower looks a bit like a rocket about to blast off into space. In fact, the fins were intended to keep the tower itself from being blasted by a furious Gulf hurricane. Just such a storm struck the station in 1886, and when it had passed, nothing but the tower remained. The stout buttresses had saved it.

The primary reason for the tower's unusual design was the fact that it stood on unstable, marshy ground only about three feet above sea level. Army engineer Danville Leadbetter, later a Confederate general, gave the tower its fat fins in order to distribute its weight over what was, in effect, an extra-wide foundation. Apparently, Leadbetter's experiment succeeded, since the tower still stands more than 140 years after it was built.

That the lighthouse was built at all was something of a historical accident. During the mid-nineteenth century, the Sabine River was a little-used backwater. The placement of a major and, as it turned out, very expensive seamark near the river was due largely to pressure applied by local politicians. They wanted to see the federal government demonstrate its commitment to the Lone Star State, which had only recently entered the Union. Hoping to reassure the nation's new Texas brethren, Congress appropriated $30,000 for the project. Despite the availability of this sizable sum as early as 1851, the station was not completed and ready for duty for almost six years. The lamps inside its third-order Fresnel lens were finally lit in April 1857. They would burn for only four years before coastal fighting darkened them for the duration of the Civil War.

Several sharp Civil War engagements were fought within sight of the tower. At one time or another it was used as a lookout or watchtower for land or naval forces on both sides. On several occasions Union landing parties were driven back in pitched battles near the station. During a major Union assault on the Sabine in 1863, Confederate defenders threw federal troops back in a fierce engagement in the very shadow of the tower.

Relit following the war, the station served until the Coast Guard discontinued it in 1952. Plans to make the lighthouse part of a Louisiana state park eventually fizzled. Today the tower is privately owned.

HOW TO GET THERE:

Located on private land, the lighthouse is accessible only by boat. However, it can be seen from the town of Sabine Pass on the Texas side of the Sabine River. For information call the Port Arthur Visitors' Bureau at (800) 235–7822 or contact the Beaumont Convention and Visitors' Bureau, 801 Main Street, Suite 100, P.O. Box 3827, Beaumont, TX 77704; (409) 880–3749. While in the area be sure to visit the Sea Rim State Park just to the southwest of Sabine Pass. The park's scenery and wildlife offer a glimpse of Texas as it must have looked 150 years ago. For information write to Sea Rim State Park, P.O. Box 1066, Sabine Pass, TX 77655; (409) 971–2559.

(Photo by Bob and Sandra Shanklin)

SABINE BANK LIGHT

Gulf of Mexico off Sabine, Texas – 1906

The Sabine River, which empties into the Gulf at the border of Louisiana and Texas, was once a sleepy, backcountry waterway. By the end of the nineteenth century, however, increasing numbers of deep-water freighters were visiting docks at Port Arthur and elsewhere along the river. Dredged and deepened channels had made the Sabine an inland highway for oceangoing vessels. To reach the river safely, however, ships had to steer clear of the Sabine Bank, a major shoal lurking twenty feet below the surface about fifteen miles from shore.

To warn ships of the danger, a light station was built directly over the shoal. Because of the water's depth, officials opted for a caisson-type, rather than screw-pile structure, affording a much more secure foundation for the lighthouse. While the caisson was being placed, a pressurized chamber allowed the construction crew to work well below the surface. Once the caisson was filled with concrete, it served as a platform for a prefabricated, tank-like iron tower assembled at a Detroit, Michigan, foundry. Lamps inside the station's third-order Fresnel lens were first lit on March 15, 1906.

The light's keepers were forced to remain at the isolated station for weeks or even months at a time. While on duty, they lived inside the cylindrical tower, only about thirty feet in diameter, and had little or no contact with the outside world. The station's crew survived a major hurricane in 1915, when huge waves rolled completely over the tower. Despite the pounding, they never allowed the light to go out.

An acetylene lighting system replaced the original Fresnel lens in 1923, when the light was automated. Although nowadays the old lighthouse stands guard over the shoal alone, its beacon remains in service.

HOW TO GET THERE:

Still an active aid to navigation, the Sabine Bank Lighthouse is off-limits to the public. Located in the open Gulf of Mexico about 15 miles from the coast, it can be reached only by boat. For information contact the Beaumont Convention and Visitors' Bureau, 801 Main Street, Suite 100, P.O. Box 3827, Beaumont, TX 77704; (409) 880–3749 or call the Port Arthur Visitors' Bureau at (800) 235–7822.

Battered by wind, water, and time, the Sabine Bank tower suggests an ancient hulk raised from the deep. (Photo by Bob and Sandra Shanklin)

BOLIVAR POINT LIGHT

Near Galveston, Texas – 1852 and 1872

Built in 1852, the original Bolivar Point Light was constructed of cast-iron sections that raised the lantern more than one-hundred feet above sea level. When the Civil War broke out, the Confederates pulled down the tower and reforged the iron, apparently using it to make weapons. Reconstruction of the lighthouse following the war was cut short by a yellow-fever epidemic that caused the government to place several hundred miles of the Texas coast under quarantine.

The new lighthouse, erected at a cost of more than $50,000 by work crews brought in from New Orleans, was not completed until late 1872. Like its predecessor and the lighthouse at Biloxi, the tower had an iron shell. This greatly increased the strength of the tower, enabling it to survive numerous gales, such as the disastrous hurricane in 1900 (described in the introduction to this chapter).

In 1915 another hurricane bore down on Galveston, and once more, the Bolivar Point Lighthouse became a refuge. This time about sixty people climbed onto the tower steps to escape the wind and the flood tide accompanying the storm. The flood carried away the tank containing the oil supply for the lamps so that the light was extinguished for two critical days following the storm.

Discontinued by the Coast Guard in 1933, the Bolivar Point Light has been dark now for more than half a century.

HOW TO GET THERE:

Now privately owned and closed to the public, the tower can be seen from State 87 on the Bolivar Peninsula. To reach the peninsula, take the free ferry from the north end of Galveston Island. The ferry provides an excellent view of the lighthouse.

The Bolivar Point Light survived a severe hurricane on the Gulf of Mexico in 1900.

(Courtesy U.S. Coast Guard)

GALVESTON JETTY LIGHT

Galveston, Texas – 1918

Begun in 1905, the Galveston Jetty Lighthouse took more than thirteen years to build. Construction was delayed by the infamous Galveston hurricane and flood of 1906 and by later storms that repeatedly bent and twisted pilings into unrecognizable junk iron. Finally completed in 1918, the station remained dark until after the end of World War I because of the threat of German U-boats. It was automated in 1973.

A two-masted sailing ship capsized and shattered by the 1906 Galveston hurricane. (Galveston Texas Flood Stereograph, from Center for American History University of Texas at Austin)

HALFMOON REEF LIGHT

Port Lavaca, Texas – 1858

The Halfmoon Reef Lighthouse once stood on pilings in the middle of Matagorda Bay. Today it sits on land beside the Chamber of Commerce building in Port Lavaca, Texas.

Erected in 1858, the lighthouse warned ships away from the dangerous Halfmoon Reef in Matagorda Bay. Although located over open water, it survived countless storms, including major hurricanes in 1864, 1875, and 1886. It took a truly calamitous hurricane in 1942 to put it out of service.

The following year the lighthouse narrowly missed being blown to bits by a flight of World War II bombers. A crew had just arrived to load the sagging structure onto a barge—it had been knocked off its pilings by the hurricane—and move it to land. The crew was still hard at work when a Coast Guard vessel pulled alongside with some alarming news. In less than thirty minutes

the area was scheduled for use as a bombing range. Luckily, the Coast Guard managed to wave off the airplanes before they dropped their explosives.

For many years the Halfmoon Reef Lighthouse sat dilapidated and abandoned at the Point Comfort dredging yard. But in 1979 it was moved overland to Port Lavaca where, instead of a coastal mark, it is now a landmark. The lighthouse retains its distinction, as its steps have become a popular place for weddings.

HOW TO GET THERE:

Originally located in Matagorda Bay at the tip of Halfmoon Reef, the lighthouse now stands on State 35 at Port Lavaca. For more information, contact the Port Lavaca–Calhoun County Chamber of Commerce (located next door to the lighthouse), Box 528, Port Lavaca, Texas 77979; (512) 552–1234.

Now part of a Chamber of Commerce complex in Port Lavaca, the Halfmoon Reef Lighthouse once stood on pilings in Matagorda Bay.

MATAGORDA LIGHT

Matagorda Island, Texas – 1852 and 1873

The government built several lighthouses along the Texas coast in 1852, including those at Bolivar Point and Matagorda Bay. The Matagorda Lighthouse had a cast-iron tower much like the one at Bolivar, raising the lens ninety-one feet above the entrance to Matagorda Bay. Sailors had no trouble distinguishing it from other coastal towers since it was painted in red, white, and black horizontal bands.

During the early 1860s Confederate soldiers stole the lens and apparatus and buried them in the sand. Their attempt to blow up the lighthouse with kegs of gunpowder severely damaged the tower but did not topple it. Where the rebels failed, however, erosion and neglect succeeded. In 1867 the tower had to be dismantled to keep it from falling over on its own. The Lighthouse Board then rebuilt the lighthouse some two miles from its original site and had it back in service by 1873.

A powerful storm battered the Matagorda Lighthouse for two days during the late summer of 1886. Wind shook the tower so hard that a piece of the lens fell out and smashed on the floor of the lantern. Except for the tower itself and the keeper's house, wind and water swept away everything. Fortunately, the keeper had the foresight to store twenty gallons of fuel inside the tower, so that he was able to keep the light burning.

The light still burns today, marking the man-made ship channel through Pass Cavallo and into Matagorda Bay. It can be seen by the pilots of ships from as far as twenty-five miles at sea.

HOW TO GET THERE:

This lighthouse can be reached only by charter boat. For more information contact the Friends of Matagorda Island, Box 1099, Port Lavaca, Texas 77979; (512) 552–2803.

The impressive black tower of the Matagorda Lighthouse rises above grasslands at the edge of the bay.

ARANSAS PASS (LYDIA ANN) LIGHT

Port Aransas, Texas – 1857

During the nineteenth century ships headed for Corpus Christi often approached this south Texas port city through Aransas Pass. Breaking through an almost solid wall of barrier islands, the pass confronted navigators with rolling surf, uncharted shoals, and channels that seemed to shift with every tide.

In 1855 the Lighthouse Board handed the task of marking the pass over to Captain Danville Leadbetter, an Army engineer. Leadbetter built a fifty-foot octagonal brick tower and an adjacent wood-frame keeper's dwelling. Having received a fourth-order Fresnel lens, the station began operation late in 1857. Ironically, only a few years later the station's builder would be fighting against the same government he had served so dutifully as an engineer—as General Leadbetter of the Confederate Army.

General Leadbetter survived the great war that killed so many and destroyed so much of the South; the lighthouse he had designed for Aransas Pass almost did not. Its lens was removed by the Confederates and, according to an unlikely local legend, buried in the island marshes. Union warships blockading the pass literally used the tower for target practice.

After the war federal agents discovered a set of crates in Indianola, Texas, containing a fourth-order Fresnel lens, likely the one removed from the Aransas pass station—so much for legends. The lighthouse was fully restored and back in operation by 1867, after which it served mariners more or less without interruption for more than eighty years. But by the mid-twentieth century, the spreading channel and changes in the shoreline had placed the lighthouse more than a mile from the entrance of the pass where it was most needed. In 1952 the Coast Guard replaced the light with an automated beacon located on the opposite shore of Aransas Pass.

In 1970 the Coast Guard sold the historic station to a private owner, who, as it turned out, was a lover of classic lighthouses. The Aransas Pass Lighthouse was restored to prime condition and eventually relit as an official aid to navigation. The light is shown on charts as the Lydia Ann Light, after the Lydia Ann Channel that runs close to the northeastern shore of the pass.

HOW TO GET THERE:

The lighthouse property is privately owned and not open to the public, but both the tower and its light—visible from about 7 miles away—can be seen from boats in the nearby Lydia Ann Channel. The original Fresnel lens that once shined here is on display in the Port Aransas Civic Center. To reach Port Aransas follow Route 35 North from Corpus Christi, then Route 361 toward Mustang Island. For more information contact the Port Aransas Chamber of Commerce at P.O. Box 356, Port Aransas, TX 78373; (512) 749–5919.

(Courtesy U.S. Coast Guard)

POINT ISABEL LIGHT

Point Isabel, Texas – 1852

Also constructed in 1852, a good year for lighthouses in Texas, the Point Isabel Light was erected on an old army camp used by the forces of General Zachary Taylor during the Mexican War. The site also attracted considerable military interest during the Civil War. Both the Confederate and Union forces used the tower as an observation post, and on May 13, 1865, the two sides fought each other at Palmito Ranch, almost within a rifle shot of the lighthouse. The Southerners won the battle but discovered, to their dismay, that they had already lost the war. Robert E. Lee had surrendered at Appomattox Courthouse in Virginia more than a month earlier.

Sea traffic in the vicinity of Port Isabel began to decline after the war, and in 1888 the Lighthouse Board discontinued the light. A few years later, when board members voted to re-exhibit the light, they were very surprised to learn that the government no longer owned the lighthouse. Technically speaking, the government had never owned Point Isabel itself. It seems that General Taylor had not purchased the land but had illegally expropriated it for the use of his army. After years of litigation and negotiation, the board ended up having to buy back its own lighthouse from a Texas rancher for $6,000.

Shortly after the turn of the century, the Point Isabel Light fell permanently dark. Although not used for more than eighty years, it remains in excellent condition, the centerpiece, in fact, of Texas's smallest state park.

HOW TO GET THERE:

The lighthouse stands on a hill beside State 100 just east of the junction with State 48 in the center of Port Isabel. The state of Texas maintains the lighthouse. There are self-guided tours daily.

For more information contact the Texas Parks and Wildlife Department, 4200 Smith School Road, Austin, Texas 78744; (210) 943–1172.

Point Isabel Light has stood for nearly 150 years.

LIGHTHOUSES INDEX

Numerals in italics indicate photograph/legend only.

BIBLIOGRAPHY

Adams, William Henry Davenport. *Lighthouses and Lightships: A Descriptive and Historical Account of Their Mode of Construction and Organization.* New York: Scribner's, 1870.

Buehr, Walter. *Storm Warning: The Story of Hurricanes and Tornadoes.* New York: Morrow, 1972.

Cipra, David L. *Lighthouses and Lightships of the Gulf of Mexico.* U.S. Coast Guard, 1978.

Dean, Love. *Reef Lights: Seaswept Lighthouses of the Florida Keys.* Key West: The Historic Key West Preservation Board, 1982.

De Wire, Elinore. *Florida Lighthouses.*

Holland, Francis Ross, Jr. *America's Lighthouses: Their Illustrated History Since 1716.* Brattleboro, Vt.: Stephen Greene Press, 1972.

Marx, Robert. *Shipwrecks of the Western Hemisphere.* New York: David McKay Company, 1971.

Mason, Herbert Mollow. *Death from the Seas: The Galveston Hurricane of 1900.* New York: Dial, 1972.

Moe, Christine. *Lighthouses and Lightships.* Monticello, Ill.: 1979.

Naush, John M. *Seamarks: Their History and Development.* London: Stanford Maritime, 1985.

Scheina, Robert L. "The Evolution of the Lighthouse Tower," *Lighthouses: Then and Now* (supplement to the U.S. Coast Guard Commandant's Bulletin).

Simpson, Robert. *The Hurricane and Its Impact.* Baton Rouge: Louisiana State University, 1980.

Snowe, Edward Rowe, *Famous Lighthouses of America.* New York: Dodd, Mead, 1955.

——— *Great Gales and Dire Disasters.* New York: Dodd, Mead, 1952.

FOR FURTHER INFORMATION
ON LIGHTHOUSES

Lighthouse Preservation Society
P.O. Box 736
Rockport, MA 01966

Lighthouse Digest
P.O. Box 1690
Wells, ME 04090
(207) 646–0515

U.S. Lighthouse Society
244 Kearney Street, 5th Floor
San Francisco, CA 94108

U.S. Coast Guard
Historian's Office
2100 2nd Street, SW
Washington, D.C. 20593

National Archives
Record Group 26
Washington, D.C. 20480

*Record Group 26 constitutes the records of the Bureau of
Lighthouses 1789–1939 as well as U.S. Coast Guard records
1828–1947.*

National Park Service
Maritime Initiative
P.O. Box 37127
Washington, D.C. 20013

ABOUT THE AUTHORS

BRUCE ROBERTS and his wife, Cheryl, who helped with the research for this book, live on North Carolina's Outer Banks, not far from the Bodie Island Lighthouse. For many years Bruce was Senior Travel Photographer for *Southern Living* magazine. He started his career working as a photographer for newspapers in Tampa, Florida, and Charlotte, North Carolina. He is the recipient of many photography awards, and some of his photos are in the permanent collection of the Smithsonian Institution. Recently Bruce and Cheryl opened the Lighthouse Gallery & Gifts, a store devoted to lighthouse books, artifacts, and collectibles, in Nags Head.

RAY JONES is a freelance writer and publishing consultant living in Surry, a small town on the coast of Maine. He began his writing career working as a reporter for weekly newspapers in Texas. He has served as an editor for Time-Life Books, as founding editor of *Albuquerque Living* magazine, as a senior editor and writing coach at *Southern Living* magazine, and as founder and publisher of Country Roads Press. Ray grew up in Macon, Georgia, where he was inspired by the writing of Ernest Hemingway and William Faulkner.